William Mason

The English Garden, a Poem in Four Books

A New Edition

William Mason

The English Garden, a Poem in Four Books
A New Edition

ISBN/EAN: 9783744771481

Printed in Europe, USA, Canada, Australia, Japan

Cover: Foto ©Thomas Meinert / pixelio.de

More available books at **www.hansebooks.com**

THE

ENGLISH GARDEN:

A

POEM.

IN

FOUR BOOKS.

By W. MASON, M. A.

A NEW EDITION, corrected.

To which are added

A

COMMENTARY and NOTES,

By W. BURGH, Esq; LL. D.

A GARDEN IS THE PUREST OF HUMAN PLEASURES; IT IS THE GREATEST REFRESHMENT TO THE SPIRITS OF MAN, WITHOUT WHICH BUILDINGS AND PALACES ARE BUT GROSS HANDY-WORKS. AND A MAN SHALL EVER SEE, THAT WHEN AGES GROW TO CIVILITY AND ELEGANCE, MEN COME TO BUILD STATELY, SOONER THAN TO GARDEN FINELY: AS IF GARDENING WERE THE GREATER PERFECTION.

VERULAM.

YORK, PRINTED BY A. WARD:

And sold by J. DODSLEY, Pall-Mall; T. CADELL, in the Strand; and R. FAULDER, in New Bond-Street, London; and J. TODD, in York. 1783.

PREFACE.

AS the Four Books, which compoſe the following Poem, were publiſhed originally at very diſtant intervals, I thought it expedient at the concluſion of the laſt to ſubjoin a Poſtſcript, in which I drew up an Analyſis of each of them in their order, that the general plan of the whole work, and their connection with one another, might be more accurately conceived. That ſhort analyſis is now withdrawn, being ſuperſeded by a copious and complete Commentary, which the partiality of a very ingenious and learned friend has induced him to write upon it; a work which I am perſuaded will be of more utility to thoſe readers, who wiſh to underſtand the ſubject, than the Poem itſelf will be of entertainment to that more numerous claſs who read merely to be entertained: For myſelf, as to amuſe was only a ſecondary motive with me when I compoſed the work, I freely own

 that

that I am more pleaſed by a ſpecies of writing which tends to elucidate the Principles of my Poem, and to develope its method, than I ſhould have been with that more flattering, yet leſs uſeful one; which intereſted itſelf in diſplaying what little poetical merit it may poſſeſs.

Notwithſtanding this; I am well aware that many perſons will think my friend has taken much more pains than were neceſſary on this occaſion; and I ſhould agree with them in opinion were the Poem only, and not the Subject which it treats, in queſtion: But I would wiſh them to diſcriminate between theſe two points, and that whatever they may think of the writer's condeſcenſion in commenting ſo largely on the one, they would give him credit for the great additional illuſtration which he has thrown upon the other.

Yet as to the Poem itſelf, I am not without my hopes, that in this new Edition I have

have rendered it somewhat more worthy of the pains which its Commentator has bestowed upon it, and of that approbation which it has already obtained from a very respectable part of the public; having revised it very carefully throughout, and purged it, to the best of my abilities, of many defects in the prior editions. That original Sin, however, which the admirers of Rhyme, and of Rhyme only, have laid to its charge, I have still ventured to retain: To this fault I must still own myself so blind, that in defence of it I shall again reprint what I said before in my former Postscript, and make it the conclusion of my present Preface.

"When I first had the subject in contemplation, I found it admitted of two very different modes of composition: One was that of the regular Didactic Poem, of which the Georgics of Virgil afford so perfect an example;

the

the other that of the preceptive epiſtolary eſſay, the model of which Horace has given in his Epiſtles *Ad Auguſtum* and *ad Piſones.* I balanced ſome time which of theſe I ſhould adopt, for both had their peculiar merit. The former opened a more ample field for pićtureſque deſcription and poetical embelliſhment; the latter was more calculated to convey exaćt precept in conciſe phraſe*. The

* See Mr. Pope's account of his *deſign* in writing the Eſſay on Man, where the peculiar merit of that way, in which he ſo greatly excelled, is moſt happily explained. He choſe, as he ſays, "Verſe, and even Rhyme, for two reaſons: Verſe, becauſe precepts, ſo written, ſtrike more ſtrongly, and are retained more eaſily: Rhyme, becauſe it expreſſes arguments or inſtrućtions more conciſely than even Proſe itſelf." As I have lately, in the Preface to my Tranſlation of Freſnoy's Art of Painting, made uſe of this very reaſon for tranſlating that Poem into Rhyme, ſome ſuperficial readers may think that I hereby contradićt myſelf; but the judicious critic will refer Freſnoy's Poem to *Horace's Art of Poetry* as to its proper architype, and rightly deem it, though not an *epiſtolary*, yet a *preceptive Eſſay*. Whereas the preſent work comes under that ſpecies of compoſition which has the *Georgics of Virgil* for its original, than which no two modes of writing can be more diſſimilar.

The one furniſhed better means of illuſtrating my ſubject, and the other of defining it; the former admitted thoſe ornaments only which reſulted from lively imagery and figurative diction; the latter ſeemed rather to require the ſeaſoning of wit and ſatire; this, therefore, appeared beſt calculated to expoſe falſe taſte, and that to elucidate the true. But falſe taſte, on this ſubject, had been ſo inimitably ridiculed by Mr. Pope, in his Epiſtle to Lord Burlington, that it ſeemed to preclude all other authors (at leaſt it precluded me) from touching it after him; and therefore, as he had left much unſaid on that part of the art on which it was my purpoſe principally to enlarge, I thought the didactic method not only more open but more proper for my attempt. This matter once determined, I did not heſitate as to my choice between blank verſe and rhyme; becauſe it clearly appeared, that numbers of the moſt varied kind were moſt proper to

illuſtrate

illuſtrate a ſubject *whoſe every charm ſprings from variety*, and which, painting Nature as *ſcorning control*, ſhould employ a verſification for that end as unfettered as Nature itſelf. Art at the ſame time, in rural improvements, pervading the province of Nature, unſeen, and unfelt, ſeemed to bear a ſtriking analogy to that ſpecies of verſe, the harmony of which reſults from meaſured quantity and varied cadence, without the too ſtudied arrangement of final ſyllables, or regular return of conſonant ſounds. I was, notwithſtanding, well aware, that by chooſing to write in blank verſe, I ſhould not court popularity, becauſe I perceived it was growing much out of vogue; but this reaſon, as may be ſuppoſed, did not weigh much with a writer, who meant to combat Faſhion in the very theme he intended to write upon; and who was alſo convinced that a mode of Engliſh verſification, in which ſo many good poems, with Paradiſe Loſt at their head, have

have been written, could either not long continue unfaſhionable; or if it did, that Faſhion had ſo completely deſtroyed Taſte, it would not be worth any writer's while, who aimed at more than the reputation of the day, to endeavour to amuſe the public."

THE ENGLISH GARDEN.

BOOK THE FIRST.

TO thee, divine SIMPLICITY! to thee,
Beſt arbitreſs of what is good and fair,
This verſe belongs. O, as it freely flows,
Give it thy powers of pleaſing: elſe in vain
It ſtrives to teach the rules, from Nature drawn,
Of import high to thoſe whoſe taſte would add
To Nature's careleſs graces; lovelieſt then,
When, o'er her form, thy eaſy ſkill has taught
The robe of Spring in ampler folds to flow.
Haſte Goddeſs! to the woods, the lawns, the vales;
That lie in rude luxuriance, and but wait
Thy call to bloom with beauty. I meanwhile,
Attendant on thy ſtate ſerene, will mark
Its faery progreſs; wake th' accordant ſtring;
And tell how far, beyond the tranſient glare
Of fickle faſhion, or of formal art,
Thy flowery works with charm perennial pleaſe.

Ye too, ye ſiſter Powers! that, at my birth,
Auſpicious ſmil'd; and o'er my cradle drop'd
Thoſe magic ſeeds of Fancy, which produce
A Poet's feeling, and a Painter's eye,
Come to your votary's aid. For well ye know
How ſoon my infant accents liſp'd the rhyme,
How ſoon my hands the mimic colours ſpread,
And vainly ſtrove to ſnatch a double wreath
From Fame's unfading laurel: fruitleſs aim;
Yet not inglorious; nor perchance devoid
Of friendly uſe to this fair argument;
If ſo, with lenient ſmiles, ye deign to chear,
At this ſad hour *, my deſolated ſoul.
For deem not ye that I reſume the ſtrain
To court the world's applauſe: my years mature
Have learn'd to ſlight the toy. No, 'tis to ſooth
That agony of heart, which they alone,
Who beſt have lov'd, who beſt have been belov'd,
Can feel, or pity; ſympathy ſevere!
Which ſhe too felt, when on her pallid lip
The laſt farewell hung trembling, and beſpoke
A wiſh to linger here, and bleſs the arms
She left for heav'n. She died, and heav'n is hers!
Be mine, the penſive ſolitary balm

* Ver. 30, Note I.

That

That recollection yields. Yes, Angel pure!
While Memory holds her ſeat, thy image ſtill
Shall reign, ſhall triumph there; and when, as now,
Imagination forms a Nymph divine
To lead the fluent ſtrain, thy modeſt bluſh,
Thy mild demeanor, thy unpractis'd ſmile
Shall grace that Nymph, and ſweet Simplicity
Be dreſs'd (Ah meek MARIA!) in thy charms.

Begin the Song! and ye of Albion's ſons
Attend; Ye freeborn, ye ingenuous few,
Who heirs of competence, if not of wealth,
Preſerve that veſtal purity of ſoul
Whence genuine taſte proceeds. To you, bleſt youths,
I ſing; whether in Academic groves
Studious ye rove; or, fraught with learning's ſtores,
Viſit the Latian plain, fond to tranſplant
Thoſe arts which Greece did, with her Liberty,
Reſign to Rome. Yet know, the art I ſing
Ev'n there ye ſhall not learn. Rome knew it not
While Rome was free: Ah! hope not then to find
In ſlaviſh ſuperſtitious Rome the fair
Remains. Meanwhile, of old and claſſic aid
Tho' fruitleſs be the ſearch, your eyes entranc'd

Shall catch thoſe glowing ſcenes, that taught a CLAUDE
To grace his canvaſs with Heſperian hues:
And ſcenes like theſe, on Memory's tablet drawn,
Bring back to Britain; there give local form
To each Idea; and, if Nature lend
Materials fit of torrent, rock, and ſhade,
Produce new TIVOLIS. But learn to rein,
O Youth! whoſe ſkill eſſays the arduous taſk,
That ſkill within the limit ſhe allows.
Great Nature ſcorns controul: ſhe will not bear
One beauty foreign to the ſpot or ſoil
She gives thee to adorn: 'tis thine alone
To mend, not change her features. Does her hand
Stretch forth a level lawn? Ah, hope not thou
To lift the mountain there. Do mountains frown
Around? Ah, wiſh not there the level lawn.
Yet ſhe permits thy art, diſcreetly us'd,
To ſmooth the rugged and to ſwell the plain.
But dare with caution; elſe expect, bold man!
The injur'd Genius of the place to riſe
In ſelf-defence, and, like ſome giant fiend
That frowns in Gothic ſtory, ſwift deſtroy,
By night, the puny labours of thy day.

What

What then muſt he attempt, whom niggard Fate
Has fixt in ſuch an inauſpicious ſpot
As bears no trace of beauty? muſt he ſit
Dull and inactive in the deſert waſte,
If Nature there no happy feature wears
To wake and meet his ſkill? Believe the Muſe,
She does not know that inauſpicious ſpot
Where Beauty is thus niggard of her ſtore:
Believe the Muſe, thro' this terreſtrial vaſt
The ſeeds of grace are ſown, profuſely ſown,
Ev'n where we leaſt may hope: the deſert hills
Will hear the call of Art; the vallies dank
Obey her juſt beheſts, and ſmile with charms
Congenial to the ſoil, and all its own.

For tell me, where's the deſert? there alone
Where man reſides not; or, if 'chance reſides,
He is not there the man his Maker form'd,
Induſtrious man, by heav'n's firſt law ordain'd
To earn his food by labour. In the waſte
Place thou that man with his primæval arms,
His plough-ſhare, and his ſpade; nor ſhalt thou long
Impatient wait a change; the waſte ſhall ſmile
With yellow harveſts; what was barren heath

Shall

Shall ſoon be verdant mead. Now let thy Art
Exert its powers, and give, by varying lines,
The ſoil, already tam'd, its finiſh'd grace.

Nor leſs obſequious to the hand of toil,
If Fancy guide that hand, will the dank vale
Receive improvement meet; but Fancy here
Muſt lead, not follow Labour; ſhe muſt tell
In what peculiar place the ſoil ſhall riſe,
Where ſink; preſcribe what form each ſluice ſhall wear,
And how direct its courſe; whether to ſpread
Broad as a lake, or, as a river pent
By fringed banks, weave its irriguous way
Thro' lawn and ſhade alternate: for if She
Preſide not o'er the taſk, the narrow drains
Will run in tedious parallel, or cut
Each other in ſharp angles; hence implore
Her ſwift aſſiſtance, ere the ruthleſs ſpade
Too deeply wound the boſom of the ſoil.

Yet, in this lowly ſite, where all that charms
Within itſelf muſt charm, hard is the taſk
Impos'd on Fancy. Hence with idle fear!
Is ſhe not Fancy? and can Fancy fail

In ſweet deluſions, in concealments apt,
And wild creative power? She cannot fail.
And yet, full oft, when her creative power,
Her apt concealments, her deluſions ſweet
Have been profuſely laviſh'd; when her groves
Have ſhot, with vegetative vigour ſtrong,
Ev'n to their wiſh'd maturity; when Jove
Has roll'd the changeful ſeaſons o'er her lawns,
And each has left a bleſſing as it roll'd:
Ev'n then, perchance, ſome vain faſtidious eye
Shall rove unmindful of ſurrounding charms
And aſk for proſpect. Stranger! 'tis not here.
Go ſeek it on ſome gariſh turret's height;
Seek it on Richmond's or on Windſor's brow;
There gazing, on the gorgeous vale below,
Applaud alike, with faſhion'd pomp of phraſe,
The good and bad, which, in profuſion, there
That gorgeous vale exhibits. Here meanwhile,
Ev'n in the dull, unſeen, unſeeing dell,
Thy taſte contemns, ſhall Contemplation imp
Her eagle plumes; the Poet here ſhall hold
Sweet converſe with his Muſe; the curious Sage,
Who comments on great Nature's ample tome,
Shall find that volume here. For here are caves,

Where riſe thoſe gurgling rills, that ſing the ſong
Which Contemplation loves; here ſhadowy glades,
Where thro' the tremulous foliage darts the ray,
That gilds the Poet's day-dream; here the turf
Teems with the vegetating race; the air
Is peopled with the inſect tribes, that float
Upon the noontide beam, and call the Sage
To number and to name them. Nor if here
The Painter comes, ſhall his enchanting art
Go back without a boon: for Fancy here,
With Nature's living colours, forms a ſcene
Which RUISDALE beſt might rival: chryſtal lakes,
O'er which the giant oak, himſelf a grove,
Flings his romantic branches, and beholds
His reverend image in th' expanſe below.
If diſtant hills be wanting, yet our eye
Forgets the want, and with delighted gaze
Reſts on the lovely foreground; there applauds
The art, which, varying forms and blending hues,
Gives that harmonious force of ſhade and light,
Which makes the landſcape perfect. Art like this
Is only art, all elſe abortive toil.

Come then, thou Siſter Muſe, from whom the mind
Wins for her airy viſions colour, form,
And fixt locality, ſweet Painting, come
To teach the docile pupil of my ſong,
How much his practice on thy aid depends.

Of Nature's various ſcenes the Painter culls
That for his fav'rite theme, where the fair whole
Is broken into ample parts, and bold;
Where to the eye three well-mark'd diſtances
Spread their peculiar colouring. Vivid green,
Warm brown, and black opake the foreground bears
Conſpicuous; ſober olive coldly marks
The ſecond diſtance; thence the third declines
In ſofter blue, or, leſs'ning ſtill, is loſt
In fainteſt purple. When thy taſte is call'd
To deck a ſcene where Nature's ſelf preſents
All theſe diſtinct gradations, then rejoice
As does the Painter, and like him apply
Thy colours; plant thou on each ſeparate part
Its proper foliage. Chief, for there thy ſkill
Has its chief ſcope, enrich with all the hues
That flowers, that ſhrubs, that trees can yield, the ſides
Of that fair path, from whence our ſight is led

Gradual to view the whole. Where'er thou wind'ſt
That path, take heed between the ſcene and eye,
To vary and to mix thy choſen greens.
Here for a while with cedar or with larch,
That from the ground ſpread their cloſe texture, hide
The view entire. Then o'er ſome lowly tuft,
Where roſe and woodbine bloom, permit its charms
To burſt upon the ſight; now thro' a copſe
Of beech, that rear their ſmooth and ſtately trunks,
Admit it partially, and half exclude,
And half reveal its graces: in this path,
How long ſoe'er the wanderer roves, each ſtep
Shall wake freſh beauties; each ſhort point preſent
A different picture, new, and yet the ſame.

Yet ſome there are who ſcorn this cautious rule,
And fell each tree that intercepts the ſcene.
O great POUSSIN! O Nature's darling, CLAUDE!
What if ſome raſh and ſacrilegious hand
Tore from your canvaſs thoſe umbrageous pines
That frown in front, and give each azure hill
The charm of contraſt! Nature ſuffers here
Like outrage, and bewails a beauty loſt,
Which Time with tardy hand ſhall late reſtore.

Yet here the ſpoiler reſts not; ſee him riſe
Warm from his devaſtation, to improve,
For ſo he calls it, yonder champian wide.
There on each bolder brow in ſhapes acute
His fence he ſcatters; there the Scottiſh fir
In murky file lifts his inglorious head,
And blots the fair horizon. So ſhould art
Improve thy pencil's ſavage dignity,
SALVATOR! if where, far as eye can pierce,
Rock pil'd on rock, thy Alpine heights retire,
She flung her random foliage, and diſturb'd
The deep repoſe of the majeſtic ſcene.
This deed were impious. Ah, forgive the thought,
Thou more than Painter, more than Poet! HE,
Alone thy equal, who was "Fancy's child."

Does then the Song forbid the Planter's hand
To clothe the diſtant hills, and veil with woods
Their barren ſummits? No, it but forbids
All poverty of clothing. Rich the robe,
And ample let it flow, that Nature wears
On her thron'd eminence: where'er ſhe takes
Her horizontal march, purſue her ſtep
With ſweeping train of foreſt; hill to hill

Unite with prodigality of ſhade.
There plant thy elm, thy cheſnut; nouriſh there
Thoſe ſapling oaks, which, at Britannia's call,
May heave their trunks mature into the main,
And float the bulwarks of her liberty:
But if the fir, give it its ſtation meet;
Place it an outguard to th' aſſailing north,
To ſhield the infant ſcions, till poſſeſt
Of native ſtrength, they learn alike to ſcorn
The blaſt and their protectors. Foſter'd thus,
The cradled hero gains from female care
His future vigor; but, that vigor felt,
He ſprings indignant from his nurſe's arms,
Nods his terrific helmet, ſhakes his ſpear,
And is that awful thing which heav'n ordain'd
The ſcourge of tyrants, and his country's pride.

If yet thy art be dubious how to treat
Nature's neglected features, turn thy eye
To thoſe, the maſters of correct deſign,
Who, from her vaſt variety, have cull'd
The lovelieſt, boldeſt parts, and new arrang'd;
Yet, as herſelf approv'd, herſelf inſpir'd.
In their immortal works thou ne'er ſhalt find

Dull uniformity, contrivance quaint,
Or labour'd littleneſs; but contraſts broad,
And careleſs lines, whoſe undulating forms
Play thro' the varied canvaſs: theſe tranſplant
Again on Nature; take thy plaſtic ſpade,
It is thy pencil; take thy ſeeds, thy plants,
They are thy colours; and by theſe repay
With intereſt every charm ſhe lent thy art.

Nor, while I thus to Imitation's realm
Direct thy ſtep, deem I direct thee wrong;
Nor aſk, why I forget great Nature's fount,
And bring thee not the bright inſpiring cup
From her original ſpring? Yet, if thou aſk'ſt,
Thyſelf ſhalt give the anſwer. Tell me why
Did RAPHAEL ſteal, when his creative hand
Imag'd the Seraphim, ideal grace
And dignity ſupernal from that ſtore
Of Attic ſculpture, which the ruthleſs Goth
Spar'd in his headlong fury? Tell me this:
And then confeſs that beauty beſt is taught
By thoſe, the favor'd few, whom Heav'n has lent
The power to ſeize, ſelect, and reunite
Her lovelieſt features; and of theſe to form

One Archetype compleat of ſovereign Grace.
Here Nature ſees her faireſt forms more fair;
Owns them for hers, yet owns herſelf excell'd
By what herſelf produc'd. Here Art and She
Embrace; connubial Juno ſmiles benign,
And from the warm embrace Perfection ſprings.

Rouſe then each latent energy of ſoul
To claſp ideal beauty. Proteus-like,
Think not the changeful Nymph will long elude
Thy chaſe, or with reluctant coyneſs frown.
Inſpir'd by Her thy happy art ſhall learn
To melt in fluent curves whate'er is ſtraight,
Acute, or parallel. For, theſe unchang'd,
Nature and ſhe diſdain the formal ſcene.
'Tis their demand, that ev'ry ſtep of Rule
Be ſever'd from their ſight: They own no charm
But thoſe that fair Variety creates,
Who ever loves to undulate and ſport
In many a winding train. With equal zeal
She, careleſs Goddeſs, ſcorns the cube and cone,
As does mechanic Order hold them dear:
Hence ſprings their enmity; and he that hopes

To

To reconcile the foes, as well might aim
With hawk and dove to draw the Cyprian car.

Such ſentence paſt, where ſhall the Dryads fly
That haunt yon antient Viſta? Pity, ſure,
Will ſpare the long cathedral iſle of ſhade
In which they ſojourn; Taſte were ſacrilege,
If, lifting there the axe, it dar'd invade
Thoſe ſpreading oaks that in fraternal files
Have pair'd for centuries, and heard the ſtrains
Of SIDNEY'S, nay, perchance, of SURRY'S reed.
Yet muſt they fall, unleſs mechanic Skill,
To ſave her offspring, rouſe at our command;
And, where we bid her move, with engine huge,
Each ponderous trunk, the ponderous trunk there move.
A work of difficulty and danger try'd,
Nor oft ſucceſsful found. But if it fails,
Thy axe muſt do its office. Cruel taſk,
Yet needful. Truſt me, tho' I bid thee ſtrike,
Reluctantly I bid thee: for my ſoul
Holds dear an antient oak, nothing more dear;
It is an antient friend. Stay then thine hand;
And try by ſaplings tall, diſcreetly plac'd
Before, between, behind, in ſcatter'd groups,

To break th' obdurate line. So may'ſt thou ſave
A choſen-few; and yet, alas, but few
Of theſe, the old protectors of the plain.
Yet ſhall theſe few give to thy opening lawn
That ſhadowy pomp, which only they can give:
For parted now, in patriarchal pride,
Each tree becomes the father of a tribe;
And, o'er the ſtripling foliage, riſing round,
Towers with parental dignity ſupreme.

And yet, My Albion! in that fair domain,
Which Ocean made thy dowry, when his love
Tempeſtuous tore thee from reluctant Gaul,
And bad thee be his Queen, there ſtill remains
Full many a lovely unfrequented wild,
Where change like this is needleſs; where no lines
Of hedge-row, avenue, or of platform ſquare
Demand deſtruction. In thy fair domain,
Yes, my lov'd Albion! many a glade is found,
The haunt of Wood-gods only: where if Art
E'er dar'd to tread, 'twas with unſandal'd foot,
Printleſs, as if the place were holy ground.
And there are ſcenes, where, tho' ſhe whilom trod,
Led by the worſt of guides, fell Tyranny,

And

And ruthlefs Superftition, we now trace
Her footfteps with delight; and pleas'd revere
What once had rous'd our hatred. But to Time,
Not her, the praife is due: his gradual touch
Has moulder'd into beauty many a tower,
Which, when it frown'd with all its battlements,
Was only terrible; and many a fane
Monaftic, which, when deck'd with all its fpires,
Serv'd but to feed fome pamper'd Abbot's pride,
And awe th' unletter'd vulgar. Generous Youth,
Whoe'er thou art, that liften'ft to my lay,
And feel'ft thy foul affent to what I fing,
Happy art thou if thou can'ft call thine own
Such fcenes as thefe: where Nature and where Time
Have work'd congenial; where a fcatter'd hoft
Of antique oaks darken thy fidelong hills;
While, rufhing thro' their branches, rifted cliffs
Dart their white heads, and glitter thro' the gloom.
More happy ftill, if one fuperior rock
Bear on its brow the fhiver'd fragment huge
Of fome old Norman fortrefs; happier far,
Ah, then moft happy, if thy vale below
Wafh, with the cryftal coolnefs of its rills,
Some mould'ring abbey's ivy-vefted wall.

O how unlike the ſcene my fancy forms,
Did Folly, heretofore, with Wealth conſpire
To plan that formal, dull, disjointed ſcene,
Which once was call'd a Garden. Britain ſtill
Bears on her breaſt full many a hideous wound
Given by the cruel pair, when, borrowing aid
From geometric ſkill, they vainly ſtrove
By line, by plummet, and unfeeling ſheers,
To form with verdure what the builder form'd
With ſtone *. Egregious madneſs; yet purſu'd
With pains unwearied, with expence unſumm'd,
And ſcience doating. Hence the ſidelong walls
Of ſhaven yew; the holly's prickly arms
Trimm'd into high arcades; the tonſile box
Wove, in moſaic mode of many a curl,
Around the figur'd carpet of the lawn.
Hence too deformities of harder cure:
The terras mound uplifted; the long line
Deep delv'd of flat canal; and all that toil,
Miſled by taſteleſs Faſhion, could atchieve
To mar fair Nature's lineaments divine.

Long was the night of error, nor diſpell'd
By Him that roſe at learning's earlieſt dawn,

* Ver. 395, Note II.

Prophet of unborn Science. On thy realm,
Philosophy! his sovereign lustre spread;
Yet did he deign to light with casual glance
The wilds of taste. Yes, sagest VERULAM, *
'Twas thine to banish from the royal groves
Each childish vanity of crisped knot
And sculptur'd foliage; to the lawn restore
Its ample space, and bid it feast the sight
With verdure pure, unbroken, unabridg'd:
For Verdure sooths the eye, as roseate sweets
The smell, or music's melting strains the ear.

So taught the Sage, taught a degenerate reign
What in Eliza's golden day was taste.
Not but the mode of that romantic age,
The age of tourneys, triumphs, and quaint masques,
Glar'd with fantastic pageantry, which dimm'd
The sober eye of truth, and dazzled ev'n
The Sage himself; witness his high-arch'd hedge,
In pillar'd state by carpentry upborn,
With colour'd mirrors deck'd, and prison'd birds.
But, when our step has pac'd his proud parterres,
And reach'd the heath, then Nature glads our eye

* Ver. 412, Note III.

Sporting in all her lovely careleſſneſs.
There ſmiles in varied tufts the velvet roſe,
There flaunts the gadding woodbine, ſwells the ground
In gentle hillocks, and around its ſides
Thro' bloſſom'd ſhades the ſecret pathway ſteals.

Thus, with a Poet's power, the Sage's pen
Pourtray'd that nicer negligence of ſcene,
Which Taſte approves. While He, delicious Swain,
Who tun'd his oaten pipe by Mulla's ſtream,
Accordant touch'd the ſtops in Dorian mood;
What time he 'gan to paint the fairy vale,
Where ſtands the Fane of Venus. Well I ween
That then, if ever, COLIN, thy fond hand
Did ſteep its pencil in the well-fount clear
Of true ſimplicity; and "call'd in Art
"Only to ſecond Nature, and ſupply
"All that the Nymph forgot, or left forlorn." *
Yet what avail'd the ſong? or what avail'd
Ev'n thine, Thou chief of Bards, whoſe mighty mind,
With inward light irradiate, mirror-like
Receiv'd, and to mankind with ray reflex
The ſov'reign Planter's primal work diſplay'd?

That

* Ver. 447, Note IV.

* That work, " where not nice Art in curious knots,
" But Nature boon pour'd forth on hill and dale
" Flowers worthy of Paradiſe; while all around
" Umbrageous grotts, and caves of cool receſs,
" And murmuring waters down the ſlope diſpers'd,
" Or held, by fringed banks, in chryſtal lakes,
" Compoſe a rural ſeat of various view."
'Twas thus great Nature's Herald blazon'd high
That fair original impreſs, which ſhe bore
In ſtate ſublime; e'er miſcreated Art,
Offspring of Sin and Shame, the banner ſeiz'd,
And with adulterate pageantry defil'd.
Yet vainly, MILTON, did thy voice proclaim
Theſe her primæval honours. Still ſhe lay
Defac'd, deflower'd, full many a ruthleſs year:
Alike, when Charles, the abject tool of France,
Came back to ſmile his ſubjects into ſlaves;
Or Belgic William, with his warriour frown,
Coldly declar'd them free; in fetters ſtill
The Goddeſs pin'd, by both alike oppreſt.

Go to the Proof! behold what TEMPLE call'd
A perfect Garden. There thou ſhalt not find
One blade of verdure, but with aching feet

* Ver. 458, Note V.

From terras down to terras ſhalt deſcend,
Step following ſtep, by tedious flight of ſtairs:
On leaden platforms now the noon-day ſun
Shall ſcorch thee; now the dank arcades of ſtone
Shall chill thy fervour; happy, if at length
Thou reach the Orchard, where the ſparing turf *
Thro' equal lines, all centring in a point,
Yields thee a ſofter tread. And yet full oft
O'er TEMPLE's ſtudious hour did Truth preſide,
Sprinkling her luſtre o'er his claſſic page:
There hear his candor own in faſhion's ſpite,
In ſpite of courtly dulneſs, hear it own
" There is a grace in wild variety
" Surpaſſing rule and order." † TEMPLE, yes,
There is a grace; and let eternal wreaths
Adorn their brows who fixt its empire here.
The Muſe ſhall hail the champions that herſelf
Led to the fair atchievement ‡. ADDISON,
Thou poliſh'd Sage, or ſhall I call thee Bard,
I ſee thee come: around thy temples play
The lambent flames of humour, bright'ning mild
Thy judgment into ſmiles; gracious thou com'ſt
With Satire at thy ſide, who checks her frown,

But

* Ver. 481, Note VI.——† Ver. 489, Note VII.
‡ Ver. 493, Note VIII.

But not her ſecret ſting. With bolder rage
Pope next advances: his indignant arm
Waves the poetic brand o'er Timon's ſhades,
And lights them to deſtruction; the fierce blaze
Sweeps thro' each kindred Viſta; Groves to Groves *
Nod their fraternal farewell, and expire.
And now, elate with fair-earn'd victory,
The Bard retires, and on the Bank of Thames
Erects his flag of triumph; wild it waves
In verdant ſplendor, and beholds, and hails
The King of Rivers, as he rolls along.
Kent is his bold aſſociate, Kent who felt
The pencil's power: † but, fir'd by higher forms
Of Beauty, than that pencil knew to paint,
Work'd with the living hues that Nature lent,
And realiz'd his Landſcapes. Generous He,
Who gave to Painting, what the wayward Nymph
Refus'd her Votary, thoſe Elyſian ſcenes,
Which would ſhe emulate, her niceſt hand
Muſt all its force of light and ſhade employ.
On thee too, Southcote, ſhall the Muſe beſtow
No vulgar praiſe: for thou to humbleſt things
Could'ſt give ennobling beauties; deck'd by thee,

The

* Ver. 503, Note IX.——† Ver. 511, Note X.

The ſimple Farm eclips'd the Garden's pride, *
Ev'n as the virgin bluſh of innocence,
The harlotry of Art. Nor, SHENSTONE, thou
Shalt paſs without thy meed, thou ſon of peace!
Who knew'ſt, perchance, to harmonize thy ſhades
Still ſofter than thy ſong; yet was that ſong
Nor rude, nor inharmonious, when attun'd
To paſtoral plaint, or tale of ſlighted love.
HIM too, the living Leader of thy powers,
Great Nature! him the Muſe ſhall hail in notes
Which antedate the praiſe true Genius claims
From juſt Poſterity: Bards yet unborn
Shall pay to BROWN that tribute, fitlieſt paid
In ſtrains, the beauty of his ſcenes inſpire.

Meanwhile, ye youths! whoſe ſympathetic ſouls
Would taſte thoſe genuine charms, which faintly ſmile
In my deſcriptive ſong, O viſit oft
The finiſh'd ſcenes, that boaſt the forming hand
Of theſe creative Genii! feel ye there
What REYNOLDS felt, when firſt the Vatican
Unbarr'd her gates, and to his raptur'd eye
Gave all the godlike energy that flow'd
From MICHAEL's pencil; feel what GARRICK felt,

* Ver. 522, Note XI.

When

When first he breath'd the soul of Shakespear's page.
So shall your Art, if call'd to grace a scene
Yet unadorn'd, with taste instinctive give
Each grace appropriate; so your active eye
Shall dart that glance prophetic, which awakes
The slumbring Wood-nymphs; gladly shall they rise
Oread, and Dryad, from their verdurous beds,
And fling their foliage, and arrange their stems,
As you, and beauty bid: the Naiad train,
Alike obsequious, from a thousand urns
Shall pour their crystaline tide; while, hand in hand,
Vertumnus, and Pomona bring their stores,
Fruitage, and flowers of ev'ry blush, and scent,
Each varied season yields; to you they bring
The fragrant tribute; ye, with generous hand
Diffuse the blessing wide, till Albion smile
One ample theatre of sylvan Grace.

END OF THE FIRST BOOK.

THE

ENGLISH GARDEN.

BOOK THE SECOND.

THE ENGLISH GARDEN.

BOOK THE SECOND.

HAIL to the Art, that teaches Wealth and Pride
How to poſſeſs their wiſh, the world's applauſe,
Unmixt with blame! that bids Magnificence
Abate its meteor glare, and learn to ſhine
Benevolently mild; like her, the Queen
Of Night, who ſailing thro' autumnal ſkies,
Gives to the bearded product of the plain
Her ripening luſtre, lingering as ſhe rolls,
And glancing cool the ſalutary ray
Which fills the fields with plenty *. Hail that Art
Ye ſwains! for, hark! with lowings glad, your herds
Proclaim its influence, wandering o'er the lawns
Reſtor'd to them and Nature; now no more
Shall Fortune's Minion rob them of their right,
Or round his dull domain with lofty wall
Oppoſe their jocund preſence. Gothic Pomp
Frowns and retires, his proud beheſts are ſcorn'd;
Now Taſte inſpir'd by Truth exalts her voice,

* Ver. 10. Note XII.

And ſhe is heard. “ Oh, let not man miſdeem;
“ Waſte is not Grandeur, Faſhion ill ſupplies
“ My ſacred place, and Beauty ſcorns to dwell
“ Where Uſe is exil'd.” At the awful ſound
The terrace ſinks ſpontaneous; on the green,
Broider'd with criſped knots, the tonſile yews
Wither and fall; the fountain dares no more
To fling its waſted cryſtal thro' the ſky,
But pours ſalubrious o'er the parched lawn
Rills of fertility. Oh beſt of Arts
That works this happy change! true Alchymy,
Beyond the Roſicruſian boaſt, that turns
Deformity to grace, expence to gain,
And pleas'd reſtores to Earth's maternal lap
The long-loſt fruits of AMALTHEA's horn.

When ſuch the theme, the Poet ſmiles ſecure
Of candid audience, and with touch aſſur'd
Reſumes his reed ASCRÆAN; eager he
To ply its warbling ſtops of various note
In Nature's cauſe, that Albion's liſtening youths,
Inform'd erewhile to ſcorn the long-drawn lines
Of ſtraight formality, alike may ſcorn
Thoſe quick, acute, perplex'd, and tangled paths,

That,

That, like the ſnake cruſh'd by the ſharpen'd ſpade,
Writhe in convulſive torture, and full oft,
Thro' many a dank and unſunn'd labyrinth,
Miſlead our ſtep; till giddy, ſpent, and foil'd,
We reach the point where firſt our race began.

These Fancy priz'd erroneous, what time Taſte,
An infant yet, firſt join'd her to deſtroy
The meaſur'd platform; into falſe extremes
What marvel if they ſtray'd, as yet unſkill'd
To mark the form of that peculiar curve,
Alike averſe to crooked and to ſtraight,
Where ſweet Simplicity reſides; which Grace
And Beauty call their own; whoſe lambent flow
Charms us at once with ſymmetry and eaſe.
'Tis Nature's curve, inſtinctively ſhe bids
Her tribes of Being trace it. Down the ſlope
Of yon wide field, ſee, with its gradual ſweep,
The ploughing ſteers their fallow ridges ſwell;
The peaſant, driving thro' each ſhadowy lane
His team, that bends beneath th' incumbent weight
Of laughing CERES, marks it with his wheel;
At night, and morn, the milkmaid's careleſs ſtep
Has, thro' yon paſture green, from ſtile to ſtile,

Impreſt

Impreſt a kindred curve; the ſcudding hare
Draws to her dew-ſprent ſeat, o'er thymy heaths,
A path as gently waving; mark them well;
Compare, pronounce, that, varying but in ſize,
Their forms are kindred all; go then, convinc'd
That Art's unerring rule is only drawn
From Nature's ſacred ſource; a rule that guides
Her ev'ry toil; or, if ſhe ſhape the path,
Or ſcoop the lawn, or, gradual, lift the hill.
For not alone to that embelliſh'd walk,
Which leads to ev'ry beauty of the ſcene,
It yields a grace, but ſpreads its influence wide,
Preſcribes each form of thicket, copſe, or wood,
Confines the rivulet, and ſpreads the lake.

Yet ſhall this graceful line forget to pleaſe,
If border'd cloſe by ſidelong parallels,
Nor duly mixt with thoſe oppoſing curves
That give the charm of contraſt. Vainly Taſte
Draws thro' the grove her path in eaſieſt bend,
If, on the margin of its woody ſides,
The meaſur'd greenſward waves in kindred flow:
Oft let the turf recede, and oft approach,
With varied breadth, now ſink into the ſhade,

Now

Now to the ſun its verdant boſom bare.
As vainly wilt thou liſt the gradual hill
To meet thy right-hand view, if to the left
An equal hill aſcends: in this, and all
Be various, wild, and free as Nature's ſelf.

For in her wildneſs is there oft an art,
Or ſeeming art, which, by poſition apt,
Arranges ſhapes unequal, ſo to ſave
That correſpondent poize, which unpreſerv'd
Would mock our gaze with airy vacancy.
Yet fair Variety, with all her powers,
Aſſiſts the Balance; 'gainſt the barren crag
She lifts the paſtur'd ſlope; to diſtant hills
Oppoſes neighb'ring ſhades; and, central oft,
Relieves the flatneſs of the lawn, or lake,
With ſtudded tuft, or iſland. So to poize
Her objects, mimic Art may oft attain:
She rules the foreground; ſhe can ſwell or ſink
Its ſurface; here her leafy ſcreen oppoſe,
And there withdraw; here part the varying greens,
And there in one promiſcuous gloom combine
As beſt befits the Genius of the ſcene.

Him then, that ſov'reign Genius, Monarch ſole
Who, from creation's primal day, derives
His right divine to this his rural throne,
Approach with meet obeiſance; at his feet
Let our aw'd art fall proſtrate. They of Ind,
The Tartar tyrants, Tamerlane's proud race,
Or they in Perſia thron'd, who ſhake the rod
Of power o'er myriads of enervate ſlaves,
Expect not humbler homage to their pride
Than does this ſylvan Deſpot *. Yet to thoſe
Who do him loyal ſervice, who revere
His dignity, nor aim, with rebel arms,
At lawleſs uſurpation, is he found
Patient and placable, receives well pleas'd
Their tributary treaſures, nor diſdains
To blend them with his own internal ſtore.

Stands he in blank and deſolated ſtate,
Where yawning crags disjointed, ſharp, uncouth,
Involve him with pale horror? In the clefts
Thy welcome ſpade ſhall heap that foſt'ring mould
Whence ſapling oaks may ſpring; whence cluſt'ring crouds
Of early underwood ſhall veil their ſides,
And teach their rugged heads above the ſhade

* Ver. 119, Note XIII.

To tower in ſhapes romantic: Nor, around
Their flinty roots, ſhall ivy ſpare to hang
Its gadding tendrils, nor the moſs-grown turf,
With wild thyme ſprinkled, there refuſe to ſpread
Its verdure. Awful ſtill, yet not auſtere,
The Genius ſtands; bold is his port, and wild,
But not forlorn, nor ſavage. On ſome plain
Of tedious length, ſay, are his flat limbs laid?
Thy hand ſhall lift him from the dreary couch,
Pillowing his head with ſwelling hillocks green,
While, all around, a foreſt-curtain ſpreads
Its waving folds, and bleſſes his repoſe.
What, if perchance in ſome prolific ſoil,
Where Vegetation ſtrenuous, uncontroll'd,
Has puſh'd her pow'rs luxuriant, he now pines
For air and freedom? Soon thy ſturdy axe,
Amid its intertwiſted foliage driv'n,
Shall open all his glades, and ingreſs give
To the bright darts of day; his priſon'd rills,
That darkling crept amid the ruſtling brakes,
Shall glitter as they glide, and his dank caves,
Free to ſalubrious Zephyrs, ceaſe to weep.
Meanwhile his ſhadowy pomp he ſtill retains,
His Dryads ſtill attend him; they alone

Of race plebeian baniſh'd, who to croud
Not grace his ſtate, their boughs obtruſive flung.

But chief conſult him ere thou dar'ſt decide
Th' appropriate bounds of Pleaſure, and of Uſe;
For Pleaſure, lawleſs robber, oft invades
Her neighbour's right, and turns to idle waſte
Her treaſures: curb her then in ſcanty bounds,
Whene'er the ſcene permits that juſt reſtraint.
The curb reſtrains not Beauty; ſov'reign ſhe
Still triumphs, ſtill unites each ſubject realm,
And bleſſes both impartial. Why then fear
Leſt, if thy fence contract the ſhaven lawn,
It does Her wrong? She points a thouſand ways,
And each her own, to cure the needful ill.
Where'er it winds, and freely muſt it wind,
She bids, at ev'ry bend, thick-bloſſom'd tufts
Croud their inwoven tendrils: is there ſtill
A void? Lo, Lebanon her Cedar lends!
Lo, all the ſtately progeny of Pines
Come, with their floating foliage richly deck'd,
To fill that void! meanwhile acroſs the mead
The wand'ring flocks that browſe between the ſhades

Seem

Seem oft to paſs their bounds; the dubious eye
Decides not if they crop the mead or lawn.

Browſe then your fill, fond Foreſters! to you
Shall ſturdy Labour quit his morning taſk
Well pleas'd; nor longer o'er his uſeleſs plots
Draw through the dew the ſplendor of his ſcythe.
He, leaning on that ſcythe, with carols gay
Salutes his fleecy ſubſtitutes, that ruſh
In bleating chace to their delicious taſk,
And, ſpreading o'er the plain, with eager teeth
Devour it into verdure. Browſe your fill
Fond Foreſters! the ſoil that you enrich
Shall ſtill ſupply your morn and evening meal
With choiceſt delicates; whether you chooſe
The vernal blades, that riſe with ſeeded ſtem
Of hue purpureal; or the clover white,
That in a ſpiked ball collects its ſweets;
Or trembling feſcue: ev'ry fav'rite herb
Shall court your taſte, ye harmleſs epicures!
Meanwhile permit that with unheeded ſtep
I paſs beſide you, nor let idle fear
Spoil your repaſt, for know the lively ſcene,
That you ſtill more enliven, to my ſoul

Darts inſpiration, and impells the ſong
To roll in bolder deſcant; while, within,
A gleam of happineſs primæval ſeems
To ſnatch me back to joys my nature claim'd,
Ere vice defil'd, ere ſlavery ſunk the world,
And all was faith and freedom: Then was man
Creation's king, yet friend; and all that browſe,
Or ſkim, or dive, the plain, the air, the flood,
Paid him their liberal homage; paid unaw'd
In love accepted, ſympathetic love
That felt for all, and bleſt them with its ſmiles.
Then, nor the curling horn had learn'd to ſound
The ſavage ſong of chace; the barbed ſhaft
Had then no poiſon'd point; nor thou, fell tube!
Whoſe iron entrails hide the ſulphurous blaſt,
Satanic engine, knew'ſt the ruthleſs power
Of thundering death around thee. Then alike
Were ye innocuous thro' your ev'ry tribe,
Or brute, or reptile; nor by rage or guile
Had giv'n to injur'd man his only plea
(And that the tyrant's plea *) to work your harm.
Inſtinct, alas, like wayward Reaſon, now
Veers from its pole. There was a golden time
When each created being kept its ſphere

* Ver. 222, Note XIV.

Appointed, nor infring'd its neighbour's right.
The flocks, to whom the graſſy lawn was giv'n,
Fed on its blades contented ; now they cruſh
Each ſcion's tender ſhoots, and, at its birth,
Deſtroy, what, ſav'd from their remorſeleſs tooth,
Had been the tree of Jove. Ev'n while I ſing,
Yon wanton lamb has cropt the woodbine's pride,
That bent beneath a full-blown load of ſweets,
And fill'd the air with perfume ; ſee it falls ;
The buſy bees, with many a murmur ſad,
Hang o'er their honied loſs. Why is it thus ?
Ah, why muſt Art defend the friendly ſhades
She rear'd to ſhield you from the noontide beam ?
Traitors, forbear to wound them ! ſay, ye fools !
Does your rich herbage fail ? do acrid leaves
Afford you daintier food ? I plead in vain ;
For now the father of the fleecy troop
Begins his devaſtation, and his ewes
Croud to the ſpoil, with imitative zeal.

Since then, conſtrain'd, we muſt expel the flock
From where our ſaplings riſe, our flow'rets bloom,
The ſong ſhall teach, in clear preceptive notes,
How beſt to frame the Fence, and beſt to hide

All its foreſeen defects; defective ſtill,
Tho' hid with happieſt art. Ingrateful ſure
When ſuch the theme, becomes the Poet's taſk:
Yet muſt he try, by modulation meet
Of varied cadence, and ſelected phraſe,
Exact yet free, without inflation bold,
To dignify that theme, muſt try to form
Such magic ſympathy of ſenſe with ſound
As pictures all it ſings; while Grace awakes
At each bleſt touch, and, on the lowlieſt things,
Scatters her rainbow hues.—The firſt and beſt
Is that, which, ſinking from our eye, divides,
Yet ſeems not to divide the ſhaven lawn,
And parts it from the paſture; for if there
Sheep feed, or dappled deer, their wandering teeth
Will, ſmoothly as the ſcythe, the herbage ſhave,
And leave a kindred verdure. This to keep
Heed that thy labourer ſcoop the trench with care;
For ſome there are who give their ſpade repoſe,
When broad enough the perpendicular ſides
Divide, and deep deſcend: To form perchance
Some needful drain, ſuch labour may ſuffice,
Yet not for beauty: here thy range of wall
Muſt lift its height erect, and, o'er its head

A verdant veil of ſwelling turf expand,
While ſmoothly from its baſe with gradual eaſe
The paſture meets its level, at that point
Which beſt deludes our eye, and beſt conceals
Thy lawn's brief limit. Down ſo ſmooth a ſlope
The fleecy foragers will gladly browſe;
The velvet herbage free from weeds obſcene
Shall ſpread its equal carpet, and the trench
Be paſture to its baſe. Thus form thy fence
Of ſtone, for ſtone alone, and pil'd on high,
Beſt curbs the nimble deer, that love to range
Unlimited; but where tame heifers feed,
Or innocent ſheep, an humbler mound will ſerve
Unlin'd with ſtone, and but a green-ſwerd trench.
Here midway down, upon the nearer bank
Plant thy thick row of thorns, and, to defend
Their infant ſhoots, beneath, on oaken ſtakes,
Extend a rail of elm, ſecurely arm'd
With ſpiculated pailing, in ſuch ſort
As, round ſome citadel, the engineer
Directs his ſharp ſtoccade. But when the ſhoots
Condenſe, and interweave their prickly boughs
Impenetrable, then withdraw their guard,
They've done their office; ſcorn thou to retain,

What frowns like military art, in ſcenes,
Where Peace ſhould ſmile perpetual. Theſe deſtroy'd,
Make it thy vernal care, when April calls
New ſhoots to birth, to trim the hedge aſlaunt,
And mould it to the roundneſs of the mound,
Itſelf a ſhelving hill; nor need we here
The rule or line preciſe, a caſual glance
Suffices to direct the careleſs ſheers.

Yet learn, that each variety of ground
Claims its peculiar barrier. When the foſs
Can ſteal tranſverſe before the central eye,
'Tis duly drawn; but, up yon neighb'ring hill
That fronts the lawn direct, if labour delve
The yawning chaſm, 'twill meet, not croſs our view;
No foliage can conceal, no curve correct
The deep deformity. And yet thou mean'ſt
Up yonder hill to wind thy fragrant way,
And wiſely doſt thou mean; for its broad eye
Catches the ſudden charms of laughing vales,
Rude rocks and headlong ſtreams, and antique oaks
Loſt in a wild horizon; yet the path
That leads to all theſe charms expects defence:
Here then ſuſpend the ſportſman's hempen toils,

And

And ſtretch their meſhes on the light ſupport
Of hazel plants, or draw thy lines of wire
In fivefold parallel; no danger then
That ſheep invade thy foliage. To thy herds,
And paſtur'd ſteeds an opener fence oppoſe,
Form'd by a triple row of cordage ſtrong,
Tight drawn the ſtakes between. The ſimple deer
Is curb'd by mimic ſnares; the ſlendereſt twine *
(If Sages err not) that the Beldame ſpins
When by her wintry lamp ſhe plies her wheel,
Arreſts his courage; his impetuous hoof,
Broad cheſt, and branching antlers nought avail;
In fearful gaze he ſtands; the nerves that bore
His bounding pride o'er lofty mounds of ſtone,
A ſingle thread defies. Such force has Fear,
When viſionary Fancy wakes the fiend,
In brute, or man, moſt powerful when moſt vain.

Still muſt the Swain, who ſpreads theſe corded guards,
Expect their ſwift decay. The noontide beams
Relax, the nightly dews contract the twiſt.
Oft too the coward hare, then only bold
When miſchief prompts, or wintry famine pines,

* Ver. 327, Note XV.

Will quit her ruſh-grown form, and ſteal, with ear
Up-prick'd, to gnaw the toils; and oft the ram
And jutting ſteer drive their entangling horns
Thro' the frail meſhes, and, by many a chaſm,
Proclaim their hate of thraldom. Nothing brooks
Confinement, ſave degenerate Man alone,
Who deems a monarch's ſmile can gild his chains.
Tir'd then, perchance, of nets that daily claim
Thy renovating labour, thou wilt form,
With elm and oak, a ruſtic baluſtrade
Of firmeſt juncture; happy could thy toil
Make it as fair as firm; yet vain the wiſh,
Aim but to hide, not grace its formal line.

Let thoſe, who weekly, from the city's ſmoke,
Croud to each neighb'ring hamlet, there to hold
Their duſty Sabbath, tip with gold and red
The milk-white paliſades, that Gothic now,
And now Chineſe, now neither, and yet both,
Checquer their trim domain. Thy ſylvan ſcene
Would fade, indignant at the tawdry glare.

'Tis thine alone to ſeek what ſhadowy hues
Tinging thy fence may loſe it in the lawn;

And

And these to give thee Painting muſt deſcend
Ev'n to her meaneſt office; grind, compound,
Compare, and by the diſtanced eye decide.

For this ſhe firſt, with ſnowy ceruſe, joins
The ochr'ous atoms that chalybeate rills
Waſh from their mineral channels, as they glide,
In flakes of earthy gold; with theſe unites
A tinge of blue, or that deep azure gray,
Form'd from the calcin'd fibres of the vine;
And, if ſhe blends, with ſparing hand ſhe blends
That baſe metallic drug then only priz'd,
When, aided by the humid touch of Time,
It gives a Nero's or ſome tyrant's cheek,
Its precious canker. Theſe with fluent oil
Attemper'd, on thy length'ning rail ſhall ſpread
That ſober olive-green which Nature wears
Ev'n on her vernal boſom; nor miſdeem,
For that, illumin'd with the noontide ray,
She boaſts a brighter garment, therefore Art
A livelier verdure to thy aid ſhould bring.
Know when that Art, with ev'ry varied hue,
Portrays the living landſcape; when her hand
Commands the canvaſs plane to glide with ſtreams,

To wave with foliage, or with flowers to breathe,
Cool olive tints, in ſoft gradation laid,
Create the general herbage: there alone,
Where darts, with vivid force, the ray ſupreme,
Unſullied verdure reigns; and tells our eye
It ſtole its bright reflection from the ſun.

The paint is ſpread; the barrier pales retire,
Snatch'd, as by magic, from the gazer's view.
So, when the ſable enſign of the night,
Unfurl'd by miſt-impelling Eurus, veils
The laſt red radiance of declining day,
Each ſcatter'd village, and each holy ſpire
That deck'd the diſtance of the ſylvan ſcene,
Are ſunk in ſudden gloom: The plodding hind,
That homeward hies, kens not the chearing ſite
Of his calm cabbin, which, a moment paſt,
Stream'd from its roof an azure curl of ſmoke,
Beneath the ſheltering coppice, and gave ſign
Of warm domeſtic welcome from his toil.

Nor is that Cot, of which fond Fancy draws
This caſual picture, alien from our theme.
Reviſit it at morn; its opening latch,

Tho'

Tho' Penury and Toil within reſide,
Shall pour thee forth a youthful progeny
Glowing with health and beauty: (ſuch the dower
Of equal heav'n) ſee, how the ruddy tribe
Throng round the threſhold, and, with vacant gaze,
Salute thee; call the loiterers into uſe,
And form of theſe thy fence, the living fence
That graces what it guards. Thou think'ſt, perchance,
That, ſkill'd in Nature's heraldry, thy art
Has, in the limits of yon fragrant tuft,
Marſhall'd each roſe, that to the eye of June
Spreads its peculiar crimſon; do not err,
The lovelieſt ſtill is wanting; the freſh roſe
Of Innocence, it bloſſoms on their cheek,
And, lo, to thee they bear it! ſtriving all,
In panting race, who firſt ſhall reach the lawn,
Proud to be call'd thy ſhepherds. Want, alas!
Has o'er their little limbs her livery hung,
In many a tatter'd fold, yet ſtill thoſe limbs
Are ſhapely; their rude locks ſtart from their brow,
Yet, on that open brow, its deareſt throne,
Sits ſweet Simplicity. Ah, clothe the troop
In ſuch a ruſſet garb as beſt beſits
Their paſtoral office; let the leathern ſcrip

Swing at their ſide, tip thou their crook with ſteel,
And braid their hat with ruſhes, then to each
Aſſign his ſtation; at the cloſe of eve,
Be it their care to pen in hurdled cote
The flock, and when the matin prime returns,
Their care to ſet them free; yet watching ſtill
The liberty they lend, oft ſhalt thou hear
Their whiſtle ſhrill, and oft their faithful dog
Shall with obedient barkings fright the flock
From wrong or robbery. The livelong day
Meantime rolls lightly o'er their happy heads;
They baſk on ſunny hillocks, or deſport
In ruſtic paſtime, while that lovelieſt grace,
Which only lives in action unreſtrain'd,
To ev'ry ſimple geſture lends a charm.

Pride of the year, purpureal Spring! attend,
And, in the cheek of theſe ſweet innocents
Behold your beauties pictur'd. As the cloud
That weeps its moment from thy ſapphire heav'n,
They frown with cauſeleſs ſorrow; as the beam,
Gilding that cloud, with cauſeleſs mirth they ſmile.
Stay, pitying Time! prolong their vernal bliſs.
Alas! ere we can note it in our ſong,

Comes manhood's feveriſh ſummer, chill'd full ſoon
By cold autumnal care, till wintry age
Sinks in the frore ſeverity of death.

Ah! who, when ſuch life's momentary dream,
Would mix in hireling ſenates, ſtrenuous there
To cruſh the venal Hydra, whoſe fell creſts
Riſe with recruited venom from the wound!
Who, for ſo vain a conflict, would forego
Thy ſylvan haunts, celeſtial Solitude!
Where ſelf-improvement, crown'd with ſelf-content,
Await to bleſs thy votary? Nurtur'd thus
In tranquil groves, liſt'ning to Nature's voice,
That preach'd from whiſpering trees, and babbling brooks,
A leſſon ſeldom learnt in Reaſon's ſchool,
The wiſe Sidonian liv'd *: and, tho' the peſt
Of lawleſs tyranny around him rag'd;
Tho' Strato, great alone in Perſia's gold,
Uncall'd, unhallow'd by the people's choice,
Uſurp'd the throne of his brave anceſtors,
Yet was his ſoul all peace; a garden's care
His only thought, its charms his only pride.

* Ver. 470, Note XVI.

But now the conquering arms of Macedon
Had humbled Perſia. Now Phænicia's realm
Receives the Son of Ammon; at whoſe frown
Her tributary kings or quit their thrones,
Or at his ſmile retain; and Sidon, now
Freed from her tyrant, points the Victor's ſtep
To where her rightful Sov'reign, doubly dear
By birth and virtue, prun'd his garden grove.

'Twas at that early hour, when now the ſun
Behind majeſtic Lebanon's dark veil
Hid his aſcending ſplendor; yet thro' each
Her cedar-veſted ſides, his flaunting beams
Shot to the ſtrand, and purpled all the main,
Where Commerce ſaw her Sidon's freighted wealth,
With languid ſtreamers, and with folded ſails,
Float in a lake of gold. The wind was huſh'd;
And, to the beach, each ſlowly-lifted wave,
Creeping with ſilver curl, juſt kiſt the ſhore,
And ſlept in ſilence. At this tranquil hour
Did Sidon's ſenate, and the Grecian hoſt,
Led by the conqueror of the world, approach
The ſecret glade that veil'd the man of toil.

Now near the mountain's foot the chief arriv'd,
Where, round that glade, a pointed aloe ſcreen,
Entwin'd with myrtle, met in tangled brakes,
That bar'd all entrance, ſave at one low gate,
Whoſe time-disjointed arch with ivy chain'd,
Bad ſtoop the warrior train. A pathway brown
Led thro' the paſs, meeting a fretful brook,
And wandering near its channel, while it leapt
O'er many a rocky fragment, where rude Art
Had eas'd perchance, but not preſcrib'd its way.

Cloſe was the vale and ſhady; yet ere long
Its foreſt ſides retiring, left a lawn
Of ample circuit, where the widening ſtream
Now o'er its pebbled channel nimbly tript
In many a lucid maze. From the flower'd verge
Of this clear rill now ſtray'd the devious path,
Amid ambroſial tufts where ſpicy plants,
Weeping their perfum'd tears of myrrh, and nard,
Stood crown'd with Sharon's roſe; or where, apart,
The patriarch Palm his load of ſugar'd dates
Shower'd plenteous; where the Fig, of ſtandard ſtrength,
And rich Pomegranate, wrapt in dulcet pulp
Their racy ſeeds; or where the citron's bough

Bent with its load of golden fruit mature.
Meanwhile the lawn beneath the ſcatter'd ſhade
Spread its ſerene extent; a ſtately file
Of circling Cypreſs mark'd the diſtant bound.

Now, to the left, the path aſcending pierc'd
A ſmaller ſylvan theatre, yet deck'd
With more majeſtic foliage. Cedars here,
Coeval with the ſky-crown'd mountain's ſelf,
Spread wide their giant arms; whence, from a rock
Craggy and black, that ſeem'd its fountain head,
The ſtream fell headlong; yet ſtill higher roſe,
Ev'n in th' eternal ſnows of Lebanon,
That hallow'd ſpring; thence, in the porous earth
Long while ingulph'd, its cryſtal weight here forc'd
Its way to light and freedom. Down it daſh'd;
A bed of native marble pure receiv'd
The new-born Naiad, and repos'd her wave,
Till with o'er-flowing pride it ſkim'd the lawn.

Fronting this lake there roſe a ſolemn grot,
O'er which an ancient vine luxuriant flung
Its purple cluſters, and beneath its roof
An unhewn altar. Rich Sabæan gums

That altar pil'd, and there with torch of pine
The venerable Sage, now firſt deſcry'd,
The fragrant incenſe kindled. Age had ſhed
That duſt of ſilver o'er his ſable locks,
Which ſpoke his ſtrength mature beyond its prime,
Yet vigorous ſtill, for from his healthy cheek
Time had not cropt a roſe, or on his brow
One wrinkling furrow plow'd; his eagle eye
Had all its youthful lightning, and each limb
The ſinewy ſtrength that toil demands, and gives.

The warrior ſaw and paus'd: his nod withheld
The crowd at awful diſtance, where their ears,
In mute attention, drank the Sage's prayer.
"Parent of good (he cried) behold the gifts
"Thy humble votary brings, and may thy ſmile
"Hallow his cuſtom'd offering. Let the hand
"That deals in blood, with blood thy ſhrines diſtain;
"Be mine this harmleſs tribute. If it ſpeaks
"A grateful heart, can hecatombs do more?
"Parent of Good! they cannot. Purple Pomp
"May call thy preſence to a prouder fane
"Than this poor cave; but will thy preſence there
"Be more devoutly felt? Parent of Good!

" It will not. Here then, ſhall the proſtrate heart,
" That deeply feels thy preſence, lift its pray'r.
" But what has he to aſk who nothing needs,
" Save, what unaſk'd, is, from thy heav'n of heav'ns
" Giv'n in diurnal good? Yet, holy Power!
" Do all that call thee Father thus exult
" In thy propitious preſence? Sidon ſinks
" Beneath a tyrant's ſcourge. Parent of Good!
" Oh free my captive country."—Sudden here
He paus'd and ſigh'd. And now, the raptur'd crowd
Murmur'd applauſe: he heard, he turn'd, and ſaw
The King of Macedon with eager ſtep
Burſt from his warrior phalanx. From the youth,
Who bore its ſtate, the conqueror's own right hand
Snatch'd the rich wreath, and bound it on his brow.
His ſwift attendants o'er his ſhoulders caſt
The robe of empire, while the trumpet's voice
Proclaim'd him King of Sidon. Stern he ſtood,
Or, if he ſmil'd, 'twas a contemptuous ſmile,
That held the pageant honours in diſdain.
Then burſt the people's voice, in loud acclaim,
And bad him be their Father. At the word,
The honour'd blood, that warm'd him, fluſh'd his cheek;
His brow expanded; his exalted ſtep

March'd

March'd firmer; graciouſly he bow'd the head;
And was the Sire they call'd him. "Tell me, King,"
Young Ammon cried, while o'er his bright'ning form
He caſt the gaze of wonder, "how a ſoul
"Like thine could bear the toils of Penury?"
"Oh grant me, Gods!" he anſwer'd, "ſo to bear
"This load of Royalty. My toil was crown'd
"With bleſſings loſt to Kings; yet, righteous Powers!
"If to my country ye transfer the boon,
"I triumph in the loſs. Be mine the chains
"That fetter Sov'reignty; let Sidon ſmile
"With, your beſt bleſſings, Liberty and Peace."

END OF THE SECOND BOOK.

THE

THE

ENGLISH GARDEN.

BOOK THE THIRD.

THE

ENGLISH GARDEN.

BOOK THE THIRD.

CLOS'D is that curious ear, by Death's cold hand,
That mark'd each error of my carelefs ftrain
With kind feverity; to whom my Mufe
Still lov'd to whifper, what fhe meant to fing
In louder accent; to whofe tafte fupreme
She firft and laft appeal'd, nor wifh'd for praife,
Save when his fmile was herald to her fame.
Yes, thou art gone; yet Friendfhip's fault'ring tongue
Invokes thee ftill; and ftill, by Fancy footh'd,
Fain would fhe hope her GRAY attends the call.
Why then, alas! in this my fav'rite haunt,
Place I the Urn, the Buft, the fculptur'd Lyre, *
Or fix this votive tablet, fair infcrib'd
With numbers worthy thee, for they are thine?
Why, if thou hear'ft me ftill, thefe fymbols fad
Of fond memorial? Ah! my penfive foul!
He hears me not, nor ever more fhall hear
The theme his candour, not his tafte approv'd.

* Ver. 12, Note XVII.

Oft, 'ſmiling as in ſcorn,' oft would he cry,
"Why waſte thy numbers on a trivial art,
"That ill can mimic even the humbleſt charms
"Of all-majeſtic Nature?" at the word
His eye would gliſten, and his accents glow
With all the Poet's frenzy, "Sov'reign Queen!
"Behold, and tremble, while thou view'ſt her ſtate
"Thron'd on the heights of Skiddaw: call thy art
"To build her ſuch a throne; that art will feel
"How vain her beſt pretenſions. Trace her march
"Amid the purple craggs of Borrowdale;
"And try like thoſe to pile thy range of rock
"In rude tumultuous chaos. See! ſhe mounts
"Her Naiad car, and, down Lodore's dread cliff
"Falls many a fathom, like the headlong Bard
"My fabling fancy plung'd in Conway's flood;
"Yet not like him to ſink in endleſs night:
"For, on its boiling boſom, ſtill ſhe guides
"Her buoyant ſhell, and leads the wave along;
"Or ſpreads it broad, a river, or a lake,
"As ſuits her pleaſure; will thy boldeſt ſong
"E'er brace the ſinews of enervate art
"To ſuch dread daring? will it ev'n direct
"Her hand to emulate thoſe ſofter charms

"That

" That deck the banks of Dove, or call to birth
" The bare romantic craggs, and copſes green,
" That ſidelong grace her circuit, whence the rills,
" Bright in their cryſtal purity, deſcend
" To meet their ſparkling Queen? around each fount
" The haw-thorns croud, and knit their bloſſom'd ſprays
" To keep their ſources ſacred. Here, even here,
" Thy art, each active ſinew ſtretch'd in vain,
" Would periſh in its pride. Far rather thou
" Confeſs her ſcanty power, correct, controul,
" Tell her how far, nor farther, ſhe may go;
" And rein with Reaſon's curb fantaſtic Taſte."

Yes I will hear thee, dear lamented Shade,
And hold each dictate ſacred. What remains
Unſung ſhall ſo each leading rule ſelect
As if ſtill guided by thy judgment ſage;
While, as ſtill modell'd to thy curious ear,
Flow my melodious numbers; ſo ſhall praiſe,
If ought of praiſe the verſe I weave may claim,
From juſt Poſterity reward my ſong.

Erewhile to trace the path, to form the fence,
To mark the deſtin'd limits of the lawn,

The

The Muſe, with meaſur'd ſtep, preceptive, pac'd.
Now from the ſurface with impatient flight
She mounts, Sylvanus! o'er thy world of ſhade
To ſpread her pinions. Open all thy glades,
Greet her from all thy echoes. Orpheus-like,
Arm'd with the ſpells of harmony ſhe comes,
To lead thy foreſts forth to lovelier haunts,
Where Fancy waits to fix them; from the dell
Where now they lurk ſhe calls them to poſſeſs
Conſpicuous ſtations; to their varied forms
Allots congenial place; ſelects, divides,
And blends anew in one Elyzian ſcene.

Yet, while I thus exult, my weak tongue feels
Its ineffectual powers, and ſeeks in vain
That force of antient phraſe which, ſpeaking, paints,
And is the thing it ſings. Ah Virgil! why,
By thee neglected, was this lovelieſt theme
Left to the grating voice of modern reed?
Why not array it in the ſplendid robe
Of thy rich diction; and conſign the charge
To Fame thy hand-maid, whoſe immortal plume
Had born its praiſe beyond the bounds of Time?

Countleſs

Countleſs is Vegetation's verdant brood
As are the ſtars that ſtud yon cope of heaven;
To marſhal all her tribes, in order'd file
Generic, or ſpecific, might demand
His ſcience, wond'rous Swede! whoſe ample mind
Like antient Tadmor's philoſophic king,
Stretch'd from the Hyſſop creeping on the wall
To Lebanon's proudeſt cedars. Skill like this,
Which ſpans a third of Nature's copious realm,
Our art requires not, ſedulous alone
To note thoſe general properties of form,
Dimenſion, growth, duration, ſtrength, and hue,
Then firſt impreſt, when, at the dawn of time,
The form-deciding, life-inſpiring word
Pronounc'd them into being. Theſe prime marks
Diſtinctive, docile Memory makes her own,
That each its ſhadowy ſuccour may ſupply
To her wiſh'd purpoſe; firſt, with needful ſhade,
To veil whate'er of wall, or fence uncouth
Diſguſts the eye, which tyrant Uſe has rear'd,
And ſtern Neceſſity forbids to change.

Lur'd by their haſty ſhoots, and branching ſtems,
Planters there are who chuſe the race of Pine

For

For this great end, erroneous; witless they
That, as their arrowy heads assault the sky,
They leave their shafts unfeather'd: rather thou
Select the shrubs that, patient of the knife,
Will thank thee for the wound, the hardy Thorn,
Holly, or Box, Privet, or Pyracanth.
They, thickening from their base, with tenfold shade
Will soon replenish all thy judgment prun'd.

But chief, with willing aid, her glittering green
Shall England's Laurel bring; swift shall she spread
Her broad-leav'd shade, and float it fair, and wide,
Proud to be call'd an inmate of the soil.
Let England prize this daughter of the East *
Beyond that Latian plant, of kindred name,
That wreath'd the head of Julius; basely twin'd
Its flattering foliage on the traitor's brow
Who crush'd his country's freedom. Sacred tree,
Ne'er be thy brighter verdure thus debas'd!
Far happier thou, in this sequester'd bower,
To shroud thy Poet, who, with fost'ring hand,
Here bade thee flourish, and with grateful strain
Now chaunts the praise of thy maturer bloom.
And happier far that Poet, if, secure

* Ver. 123, Note XVIII.

His

His Hearth and Altars from the pilfering ſlaves
Of Power, his little eve of lonely life
May here ſteal on, bleſt with the heartfelt calm
That competence and liberty inſpire.

Nor are the plants which England calls her own
Few, or unlovely, that, with laurel join'd,
And kindred foliage of perennial green,
Will form a cloſe-knit curtain. Shrubs there are
Of bolder growth, that, at the call of Spring,
Burſt forth in bloſſom'd fragrance: Lilacs rob'd
In ſnow-white innocence, or purple pride;
The ſweet Syringa yielding but in ſcent
To the rich Orange; or the Woodbine wild
That loves to hang, on barren boughs remote,
Her wreaths of flowery perfume. Theſe beſide
Myriads, that here the Muſe neglects to name,
Will add a vernal luſtre to thy veil.

And what if chance collects the varied tribes,
Yet fear not thou but unexpected charms
Will from their union ſtart. But if our ſong
Supply one precept here, it bids retire
Each leaf of deeper dye, and lift in front

Foliage of paler verdure, ſo to ſpread
A canvaſs, which when touch'd by Autumn's hand
Shall gleam with duſky gold, or ruſſet rays.
But why prepare for her funereal hand
That canvaſs ? ſhe but comes to dreſs thy ſhades,
As lovelier victims for their wintry tomb.
Rather to flowery Spring, to Summer bright,
Thy labour conſecrate ; their laughing reign,
The youth, the manhood of the growing year,
Deſerves that labour, and rewards its pain.
Yet, heedful ever of that ruthleſs time
When Winter ſhakes their ſtems, preſerve a file
With everduring leaf to brave his arm,
And deepening ſpread their undiminiſh'd gloom.

But, if the tall defect demands a ſcreen
Of foreſt ſhade high-tow'ring, ſome broad roof
Perchance of glaring tile that guards the ſtores
Of Ceres ; or the patch'd disjointed choir
Of ſome old Fane, whoſe ſteeple's Gothic pride
Or pinnacled, or ſpir'd, would bolder riſe
' In tufted trees high boſom'd,' here allot
Convenient ſpace to plant that lofty tribe
Behind thy underwood, leſt, o'er it's head

The

The foreſt tyrants ſhake their lordly arms,
And ſhed their baleful dews. Each plant that ſprings
Holds, like the people of ſome free-born ſtate,
Its rights fair franchis'd; rooted to a ſpot
It yet has claim to air; from liberal heav'n
It yet has claim to ſunſhine, and to ſhowers:
Air, ſhowers, and ſunſhine are its liberty.

That liberty ſecur'd, a general ſhade,
Denſe and impervious, to thy wiſh ſhall riſe
To hide each form uncouth; and, this obtain'd,
What next we from the Dryad powers implore
Is Grace, is Ornament: For ſee! our lawn,
Though cloath'd with ſofteſt verdure, though reliev'd
By many a gentle fall and eaſy ſwell,
Expects that harmony of light, and ſhade,
Which foliage only gives. Come then, ye plants!
That, like the village troop when Maia dawns,
Delight to mingle ſocial; to the creſt
Of yonder brow we ſafely may conduct
Your numerous train; no eye obſtructed there
Will blame your interpos'd ſociety:
But, on the plain below, in ſingle ſtems
Diſparted, or in ſparing groups diſtinct,

Wide muſt ye ſtand, in wild, diſorder'd mood,
As if the ſeeds from which your ſcyons ſprang
Had there been ſcatter'd from the affrighted beak
Of ſome maternal bird whom the fierce Hawk
Purſued with felon claw. Her young meanwhile
Callow, and cold, from their moſs-woven neſt
Peep forth; they ſtretch their little eager throats
Broad to the wind, and plead to the lone ſpray
Their famiſh'd plaint importunately ſhrill.

Yet in this wild diſorder Art preſides,
Deſigns, corrects, and regulates the whole,
Herſelf the while unſeen. No Cedar broad
Drops his dark curtain where a diſtant ſcene
Demands diſtinction. Here the thin abele
Of lofty bole, and bare, the ſmooth-ſtem'd beech,
Or ſlender alder, give our eye free ſpace
Beneath their boughs to catch each leſſening charm
Ev'n to the far horizon's azure bound.

Nor will that ſov'reign Arbitreſs admit,
Where'er her nod decrees a maſs of ſhade,
Plants of unequal ſize, diſcordant kind,
Or rul'd by Foliation's different laws;

But

But for that needful purpoſe thoſe prefers
Whoſe hues are friendly, whoſe coëval leaves
The earlieſt open, and the lateſt fade.

Nor will ſhe, ſcorning truth and taſte, devote
To ſtrange, and alien ſoils, her ſeedling ſtems;
Fix the dank ſallow on the mountain's brow,
Or, to the moſs-grown margin of the lake,
Bid the dry pine deſcend. From Nature's laws
She draws her own: Nature and ſhe are one.

Nor will ſhe, led by faſhion's lure, ſelect,
For objects interpos'd, the pigmy race
Of ſhrubs, or ſcatter with unmeaning hand
Their offspring o'er the lawn, ſcorning to patch
With many a meagre and disjointed tuft
Its ſober ſurface: ſidelong to her path
And poliſh'd foreground ſhe confines their growth
Where o'er their heads the liberal eye may range.

Nor will her prudence, when intent to form
One perfect whole, on feeble aid depend,
And give exotic wonders to our gaze.
She knows and therefore fears the faithleſs train:

Sagely ſhe calls on thoſe of hardy claſs
Indigenous, who, patient of the change
From heat to cold which Albion hourly feels,
Are brac'd with ſtrength to brave it. Theſe alone
She plants, and prunes, nor grieves if nicer eyes
Pronounce them vulgar. Theſe ſhe calls her friends,
That veteran troop who will not for a blaſt
Of nipping air, like cowards, quit the field.

Far to the north of thy imperial towers,
Auguſta! in that wild and Alpine vale,
Thro' which the Swale, by mountain-torrents ſwell'd,
Flings his redundant ſtream, there liv'd a youth
Of poliſh'd manners; ample his domain,
And fair the ſite of his paternal dome.
He lov'd the art I ſing; a deep adept
In Nature's ſtory, well he knew the names
Of all her verdant lineage; yet that ſkill
Miſled his taſte; ſcornful of every bloom
That ſpreads ſpontaneous, from remoteſt Ind
He brought his foliage; careleſs of its coſt,
Ev'n of its beauty careleſs; it was rare,
And therefore beauteous. Now his laurel ſcreen,
With roſe and woodbine negligently wove,

Bows to the axe; the rich Magnolias claim
The ſtation; now Herculean Beeches fell'd
Reſign their rights, and warm Virginia ſends
Her Cedars to uſurp them; the proud Oak
Himſelf, ev'n He the ſov'reign of the ſhade,
Yields to the Fir that drips with Gilead's balm.
Now Albion gaze at glories not thy own!
Pauſe, rapid Swale! and ſee thy margin crown'd
With all the pride of Ganges: vernal ſhowers
Have fix'd their roots; nutricious ſummer ſuns
Favor'd their growth; and mildeſt autumn ſmil'd
Benignant o'er them: vigorous, fair, and tall,
They waſt a gale of ſpices o'er the plain.
But Winter comes, and with him watry Jove,
And with him Boreas in his frozen ſhroud;
The ſavage ſpirit of old Swale is rous'd;
He howls amidſt his foam. At the dread ſight
The Aliens ſtand aghaſt; they bow their heads.
In vain the glaſſy penthouſe is ſupply'd:
The pelting ſtorm with icy bullets breaks
Its fragile barrier; ſee! they fade, they die.

Warn'd by his error, let the Planter ſlight
Theſe ſhiv'ring rarities; or if, to pleaſe

Faſtidious

Faſtidious Faſhion, he muſt needs allot
Some ſpace for foreign foliage, let him chuſe
A ſidelong glade, ſhelter'd from eaſt and north,
And free to ſouthern and to weſtern gales;
There let him fix their ſtation, thither wind
Some devious path, that, from the chief deſign
Detach'd, may lead to where they ſafely bloom.
So in the web of epic ſong ſublime
The Bard Mæonian interweaves the charm
Of ſofter epiſode, yet leaves unbroke
The golden thread of his majeſtic theme.

What elſe to ſhun of formal, falſe, or vain,
Of long-lin'd Viſtas, or plantations quaint
Our former ſtrains have taught. Inſtruction now
Withdraws; ſhe knows her limits; knows that Grace
Is caught by ſtrong perception, not from rules;
That undreſt Nature claims for all her limbs
Some ſimple garb peculiar, which, howe'er
Diſtinct their ſize and ſhape, is ſimple ſtill:
This garb to chuſe, with clothing denſe, or thin,
A part to hide, another to adorn,
Is Taſte's important taſk; preceptive ſong
From error in the choice can only warn.

But vain that warning voice; vain ev'ry aid
Of Genius, Judgment, Fancy, to ſecure
The Planter's laſting fame: There is a power,
A hidden power, at once his friend, and foe:
'Tis Vegetation. Gradual to his groves
She gives their wiſh'd effect; and, that diſplay'd,
Oh, that her power would pauſe! but active ſtill,
She ſwells each ſtem, prolongs each vagrant bough,
And darts with unremitting vigour bold
From Grace to wild luxuriance. Happier far
Are you, ye ſons of CLAUDE! who, from the mine,
The earth, or juice of herb or flower concrete,
Mingle the maſs whence your Arcadias ſpring:
The beauteous outline of your pictur'd ſhades
Still keeps the bound you gave it; Time that pales
Your vivid hues, reſpects your pleaſing forms.
Not ſo our Landſcapes: though we paint like you,
We paint with growing colours; ev'ry year,
O'erpaſſing that which gives the breadth of ſhade
We ſought, by rude addition mars our ſcene.

Rouſe then, ye Hinds! e'er yet yon cloſing boughs
Blot out the purple diſtance, ſwift prevent
The ſpreading evil: thin the crouded glades,

While yet of ſlender ſize each ſtem will thrive
Tranſplanted: Twice repeat the annual toil;
Nor let the axe its beak, the ſaw its tooth
Refrain, whene'er ſome random branch has ſtray'd
Beyond the bounds of beauty; elſe full ſoon,
Ev'n e'er the Planter's life has paſt its prime,
Will Albion's garden frown an Indian wild.

Forboding Fears avaunt! be ours to urge
Each preſent purpoſe by what favoring means
May work its end deſign'd; why deprecate
The change that waits on ſublunary things,
Sad lot of their exiſtence? ſhall we pauſe
To give the charm of Water to our ſcene,
For that the congregated rains may ſwell
Its tide into a flood? or that yon Sun,
Now on the Lion mounted, to his noon
Impells him, ſhaking from his fiery mane
A heat may parch its channel? O, ye caves,
Deepen your dripping roofs! this feveriſh hour *
Claims all your coolneſs; in your humid cells
Permit me to forget the Planter's toil;
And, while I woo your Naiads to my aid,
Involve me in impenetrable gloom.

* Ver. 354, Note XIX.

Bleſt

Bleſt is the Man (if bliſs be human boaſt)
Whoſe fertile ſoil is waſh'd with frequent ſtreams,
And ſprings ſalubrious. He diſdains to toſs
In rainbow dews their cryſtal to the ſun;
Or ſink in ſubterranean ciſterns deep;
That ſo, through leaden ſiphons upward drawn,
Thoſe ſtreams may leap fantaſtic. He his ear
Shuts to the tuneful trifling of the Bard, *
Who trick'd a gothic theme with claſſic flowers,
And ſung of Fountains burſting from the ſhells
Of brazen Tritons, ſpouting through the jaws
'Of Gorgons, Hydras, and Chimæras dire.'

Peace to his Manes! let the Nymphs of Seine
Cheriſh his fame. Thy Poet, Albion! ſcorns,
Ev'n for a cold unconſcious element
To forge the fetters he would ſcorn to wear.
His ſong ſhall reprobate each effort vile,
That aims to force the Genius of the ſtream
Beyond his native height; or dares to preſs
Above that deſtin'd line th' unwilling wave.

Is there within the circle of thy view
Some ſedgy flat, where the late-ripen'd ſheaves

* Ver. 366, Note XX.

Stand brown with unbleſt mildew? 'tis the bed
On which an ample lake in cryſtal peace
Might ſleep majeſtic. Pauſe we yet; perchance
Some midway channel, where the ſoil declines,
Might there be delv'd, by levels duly led
In bold and broken curves: for water loves
A wilder outline than the woodland path,
And winds with ſhorter bend.* To drain the reſt
The ſhelving ſpade may toil, till wintry ſhowers
Find their free courſe down each declining bank.
Quit then the thought: a River's winding form,
With many a ſinuous bay, and Iſland green,
At leſs expence of labour and of land,
Will give thee equal beauty: ſeldom art
Can emulate that broad and bold extent
Which charms in native Lakes; and, failing there,
Her works betray their character, and name,
And dwindle into pools. Not that our ſtrain,
Faſtidious, ſhall diſdain a ſmall expanſe
Of ſtagnant fluid, in ſome ſcene confin'd,
Circled with varied ſhade, where, thro' the leaves,
The half-admitted ſunbeam trembling plays
On its clear boſom; where aquatic fowl
Of varied tribe, and varied feather ſail;

* Ver. 387, Note XXI.

And where the finny race their glittering ſcales
Unwillingly reveal: There, there alone,
Where burſts the general proſpect on our eye,
We ſcorn theſe wat'ry patches: Thames himſelf,
Seen in disjointed ſpots, where Sallows hide
His firſt bold preſence, ſeems a ſtring of pools,
A chart and compaſs muſt explain his courſe.

He, who would ſeize the River's ſov'reign charm,
Muſt wind the moving mirror through his lawn
Ev'n to remoteſt diſtance; deep muſt delve
The gravelly channel that preſcribes its courſe;
Cloſely conceal each terminating bound
By hill or ſhade oppos'd; and to its bank
Lifting the level of the copious ſtream,
Muſt there retain it. But, if thy faint ſprings
Refuſe this large ſupply, ſteel thy firm ſoul
With ſtoic pride; imperfect charms deſpiſe:
Beauty, like Virtue, knows no groveling mean.

Who but muſt pity that penurious taſte,
Which down the quick-deſcending vale prolongs,
Slope below ſlope, a ſtiff and unlink'd chain

Of flat canals; then leads the ſtranger's eye
To ſome predeſtin'd ſtation, there to catch
Their ſeeming union, and the fraud approve?
Who but muſt change that pity into ſcorn,
If down each verdant ſlope a narrow flight
Of central ſteps decline, where the ſpare ſtream
Steals trickling; or, withheld by cunning ſkill,
Hoards its ſcant treaſures, till the maſter's nod
Decree its fall: Then down the formal ſtairs
It leaps with ſhort-liv'd fury; waſting there,
Poor prodigal! what many a Summer's rain
And many a Winter's ſnow ſhall late reſtore.

Learn that, whene'er in ſome ſublimer ſcene
Imperial Nature of her headlong floods
Permits our imitation, ſhe herſelf
Prepares their reſervoir; conceal'd perchance
In neighb'ring hills, where firſt it well behoves
Our toil to ſearch, and ſtudiouſly augment
The wat'ry ſtore with ſprings and ſluices drawn
From pools, that on the heath drink up the rain.
Be theſe collected, like the Miſer's gold,
In one increaſing fund, nor dare to pour,

Down

Down thy impending mound, the bright caſcade,
Till richly ſure of its redundant fall.

That mound to raiſe alike demands thy toil,
Ere Art adorn its ſurface. Here adopt
That facile mode which His inventive powers *
Firſt plann'd, who led to rich Mancunium's mart
His long-drawn line of navigated ſtream.
Stupendous taſk! in vain ſtood tow'ring hills
Oppos'd; in vain did ample Irwell pour
Her Tide tranſverſe: he pierc'd the tow'ring hill,
He bridg'd the ample tide, and high in air,
And deep through earth, his freighted barge he bore.
This mode ſhall temper ev'n the lighteſt ſoil
Firm to thy purpoſe. Then let taſte ſelect
The unhewn fragments, that may give its front
A rocky rudeneſs; pointed ſome, that there
The frothy ſpouts may break; ſome ſlaunting ſmooth,
That there in ſilver ſheet the wave may ſlide.
Here too infix ſome moſs-grown trunks of oak
Romantic, turn'd by gelid lakes to ſtone,
Yet ſo diſpos'd as if they owed their change

To

* Ver. 452, Note XXII.

To what they now controul. Then open wide
Thy flood-gates; then let down thy torrent: then
Rejoice; as if the thund'ring Tees * himſelf
Reign'd there amid his cataracts ſublime.

And thou haſt cauſe for triumph! Kings themſelves,
With all a nation's wealth, an army's toil,
If Nature frown averſe, ſhall ne'er atchieve
Such wonders: Nature's was the glorious gift;
Thy art her menial handmaid. Liſtening youths!
To whoſe ingenuous hearts I ſtill addreſs
The friendly ſtrain, from ſuch ſevere attempt
Let Prudence warn you. Turn to this clear rill,
Which, while I bid your bold ambition ceaſe,
Runs murmuring at my ſide: O'er many a rood
Your ſkill may lead the wanderer; many a mound
Of pebbles raiſe, to fret her in her courſe
Impatient: louder then will be her ſong:
For ſhe will 'plain, and gurgle, as ſhe goes,
As does the widow'd ring-dove. Take, vain Pomp!
Thy lakes, thy long canals, thy trim caſcades,
Beyond them all true taſte will dearly prize
This little dimpling treaſure. Mark the cleft,

Through

* Ver. 471, Note XXIII.

Through which ſhe burſts to day. Behind that rock
A Naiad dwells: LINEIA is her name; *
And ſhe has ſiſters in contiguous cells,
Who never ſaw the ſun. Fond Fancy's eye,
That inly gives locality and form
To what ſhe prizes beſt, full oft pervades
Thoſe hidden caverns, where pale chryſolites,
And glittering ſpars dart a myſterious gleam
Of inborn luſtre, from the gariſh day
Unborrow'd. There, by the wild Goddeſs led,
Oft have I ſeen them bending o'er their urns,
Chaunting alternate airs of Dorian mood,
While ſmooth they comb'd their moiſt cerulean locks
With ſhells of living pearl. Yes, let me own,
To theſe, or claſſic deities like theſe,
From very childhood was I prone to pay
Harmleſs idolatry. My infant eyes
Firſt open'd on that bleak and boiſt'rous ſhore,
Where Humber weds the nymphs of Trent and Ouſe
To His, and Ocean's Tritons: thence full ſoon
My youth retir'd, and left the buſy ſtrand
To Commerce and to Care. In Margaret's grove, †
Beneath whoſe time-worn ſhade old Camus ſleeps,

 Was

* Ver. 492, Note XXIV.——† Ver. 512, Note XXV.

Was next my tranquil ſtation : Science there
Sat muſing ; and to thoſe that lov'd the lore
Pointed, with myſtic wand, to truths involv'd
In geometric ſymbols, ſcorning thoſe,
Perchance too much, who woo'd the thriſtleſs muſe.
Here, though in warbling whiſper oft I breath'd
The lay, were wanting, what young Fancy deems
The life-ſprings of her being, rocks, and caves,
And huddling brooks, and torrent-falls divine.
In queſt of theſe, at Summer's vacant hour,
Pleas'd would I ſtray, when in a northern vale,
So chance ordain'd, a Naiad ſad I found
Robb'd of her ſilver vaſe ; I ſooth'd the nymph
With ſong of ſympathy, and curſt the fiend
Who ſtole the gift of Thetis *. Hence the cauſe
Why, favour'd by the blue-ey'd ſiſterhood,
They ſooth with ſongs my ſolitary ear.

Nor is LINEIA ſilent—" Long," ſhe cries,
" Too long has Man wag'd ſacrilegious war
" With the vext elements, and chief with that,
" Which elder Thales, and the Bard of Thebes
" Held firſt of things terreſtrial ; nor miſdeem'd :
" For,

* Ver. 533, Note XXVI.

" For, when the Spirit creative deign'd to move,
" He mov'd upon the waters. O revere
" Our power: for were its vital force withheld,
" Where then were Vegetation's vernal bloom,
" Where its autumnal Wealth? but we are kind
" As powerful; O let reverence lead to love,
" And both to emulation! Not a rill,
" That winds its ſparkling current o'er the plain,
" Reflecting to the Sun bright recompenſe
" For ev'ry beam he lends, but reads thy ſoul
" A generous lecture. Not a panſy pale,
" That drinks its daily nurture from that rill,
" But breathes in fragrant accents to thy ſoul,
' So by thy pity chear'd, the languiſh'd head
' Of Poverty might ſmile.' Who e'er beheld
" Our humble train forſake their native vale
" To climb the haughty hill? Ambition, ſpeak!
" He bluſhes, and is mute. When did our ſtreams,
" By force unpent, in dull ſtagnation ſleep?
" Let Sloth unfold his arms and tell the time.
" Or, if the tyranny of Art infring'd
" Our rights, when did our patient floods ſubmit
" Without recoil? Servility retires,

" And clinks his gilded chain. O, learn from us,
" And tell it to thy Nation, British Bard!
" Uncurb'd Ambition, unresisting Sloth,
" And base Dependence are the fiends accurst
" That pull down mighty empires. If they scorn
" The awful truth, be thine to hold it dear.
" So, through the vale of life, thy flowing hours
" Shall glide serene; and, like LINEIA's rill,
" Their free, yet not licentious course fulfill'd,
" Sink in the Ocean of Eternity."

END OF THE THIRD BOOK.

THE

THE

ENGLISH GARDEN.

BOOK THE FOURTH.

THE

ENGLISH GARDEN.

BOOK THE FOURTH.

NOR yet, divine SIMPLICITY, withdraw
That aid auſpicious, which, in Art's domain,
Already has reform'd whate'er prevail'd
Of foreign, or of falſe; has led the curve
That Nature loves thro' all her ſylvan haunts;
Has ſtol'n the fence unnotic'd that arreſts
Her vagrant herds; giv'n luſtre to her lawns,
Gloom to her groves, and, in expanſe ſerene,
Devolv'd that wat'ry mirror at her foot,
O'er which ſhe loves to bend and view her charms.

And tell me Thou, whoe'er haſt new-arrang'd
By her chaſte rules thy garden, if thy heart
Feels not the warm, the ſelf-dilating glow
Of true Benevolence. Thy flocks, thy herds,
That browze luxurious o'er thoſe very plots

Which once were barren, blefs thee for the change;
The birds of Air (which thy funereal Yews
Of fhape uncouth, and leaden Sons of Earth,
Antæus and Enceladus, with clubs
Uplifted, long had frighted from the fcene)
Now pleas'd return, they perch on ev'ry fpray,
And fwell their little throats, and warble wild
Their vernal minftrelfy; to Heav'n and Thee
It is a hymn of thanks: do thou, like Heav'n,
With tutelary care reward their fong.

Ere-while the Mufe, induftrious to combine
Nature's own charms, with thefe alone adorn'd
The Genius of the Scene; but other gifts
She has in ftore, which gladly now fhe brings,
And he fhall proudly wear. Know, when fhe broke
The fpells of Fafhion, from the crumbling wreck
Of her enchantments fagely did fhe cull
Thofe reliques rich of old Vitruvian fkill,
With what the Sculptor's hand in claffic days
Made breathe in Brafs or Marble; thefe the Hag
Had purloin'd, and difpos'd in Folly's fane;
To him thefe trophies of her victory
She bears; and where his awful nod ordains

Confpicuous

Conſpicuous means to place. He ſhall direct
Her dubious judgment, from the various hoard
Of ornamental treaſures, how to chuſe
The ſimpleſt and the beſt; on theſe his ſeal
Shall ſtamp great Nature's image and his own,
To charm for unborn ages.—Fling the reſt
Back to the Beldame, bid her whirl them all
In her vain vortex, lift them now to day,
Now plunge in night, as, thro' the humid rack
Of April cloud, ſwift flits the trembling beam.

But precepts tire, and this faſtidious Age
Rejects the ſtrain didactic: Try we then
In livelier Narrative the truths to veil
We dare not dictate. Sons of Albion, hear!
The tale I tell is full of ſtrange event,
And piteous circumſtance; yet deem not ye,
If names I feign, that therefore facts are feign'd:
Nor hence refuſe (what moſt augments the charm
Of ſtoried woe) that fond credulity
Which binds th' attentive ſoul in cloſer chains.

At manhood's prime ALÇANDER's duteous tear
Fell on his Father's grave. The fair Domain,

Which then became his ample heritage,
That Father had reform'd; each line deſtroy'd
Which Belgic dulneſs plann'd; and Nature's ſelf
Reſtor'd to all the rights ſhe wiſh'd to claim.

Crowning a gradual hill his Manſion roſe
In antient Engliſh grandeur: Turrets, Spires,
And Windows, climbing high from baſe to roof
In wide and radiant rows, beſpoke its birth
Coëval with thoſe rich cathedral fanes,
(Gothic ill-nam'd) where harmony reſults
From diſunited parts; and ſhapes minute,
At once diſtinct and blended, boldly form
One vaſt majeſtic whole. No modern art
Had marr'd with miſplac'd ſymmetry the Pile.
ALCANDER held it ſacred: On a height,
Which weſtering to its ſite the front ſurvey'd,
He firſt his taſte employ'd: for there a line
Of thinly ſcatter'd Beech too tamely broke
The blank Horizon. "Draw we round yon knowl,"
ALCANDER cry'd, "in ſtately Norman mode,
"A wall embattled; and within its guard
"Let every ſtructure needful for a Farm
"Ariſe in Caſtle-ſemblance; the huge Barn

"Shall

" Shall with a mock Portcullis arm the gate,
" Where Ceres entering, o'er the flail-proof floor
" In golden triumph rides; ſome Tower rotund
" Shall to the Pigeons and their callow young
" Safe rooſt afford; and ev'ry buttreſs broad,
" Whoſe proud projection ſeems a maſs of ſtone,
" Give ſpace to ſtall the heifer, and the ſteed.
" So ſhall each part, tho' turn'd to rural uſe,
" Deceive the eye with thoſe bold feudal forms
" That Fancy loves to gaze on." This atchiev'd
Now nearer home he calls returning Art
To hide the ſtructure rude where Winter pounds
In conic pit his congelations hoar,
That Summer may his tepid beverage cool
With the chill luxury; his Dairy too
There ſtands of form unſightly: both to veil,
He builds of old disjointed moſs-grown ſtone
A time-ſtruck Abbey * An impending grove
Screens it behind with reverential ſhade;
While bright in front the ſtream reflecting ſpreads,
Which winds a mimic River o'er his Lawn.
The Fane conventual there is dimly ſeen,
The mitred Window, and the Cloiſter pale,
With many a mouldering Column; Ivy ſoon

* Ver. 101, Note XXVII.

Round the rude chinks her net of foliage ſpreads ;
Its verdant meſhes ſeem to prop the wall.

One native Glory, more than all ſublime,
ALCANDER's ſcene poſſeſt : 'Twas Ocean's ſelf——
He, boiſt'rous King, againſt the eaſtern cliffs
Daſh'd his white foam ; a verdant vale between
Gave ſplendid ingreſs to his world of waves.
Slaunting this vale the mound of that clear ſtream
Lay hid in ſhade, which ſlowly lav'd his Lawn :
But there ſet free, the rill reſum'd its pace,
And hurried to the Main. The dell it paſt
Was rocky and retir'd : Here Art with eaſe
Might lead it o'er a Grot, and filter'd there,
Teach it to ſparkle down its craggy ſides,
And fall and tinkle on its pebbled floor.
Here then that Grot he builds, and conchs with ſpars,
Moſs petrified with branching corallines
In mingled mode arranges : All found here
Propriety of place ; what view'd the Main
Might well the ſhelly gifts of Thetis bear.
Not ſo the inland cave : with richer ſtore
Than thoſe the neighb'ring mines and mountains yield
To hang its roof, would ſeem incongruous Pride,
And fright the local Genius from the ſcene. *

* Ver. 131, Note XXVIII.

One vernal morn, as urging here the work
Surrounded by his hinds, from mild to cold
The Seaſon chang'd, from cold to ſudden ſtorm,
From ſtorm to whirlwind. To the angry main
Swiftly he turns and ſees a laden Ship
Diſmaſted by its rage. "Hie, hie we all,"
ALCANDER cry'd, "quick to the neighb'ring beach."
They flew; they came, but only to behold,
Tremendous ſight! the Veſſel daſh its poop
Amid the boiling breakers. Need I tell
What ſtrenuous Arts were us'd, when all were us'd,
To ſave the ſinking Crew? One tender Maid
Alone eſcap'd, ſav'd by ALCANDER's arm,
Who boldly ſwam to ſnatch her from the plank
To which ſhe feebly clung; ſwiftly to ſhore,
And ſwifter to his home the youth convey'd
His clay-cold prize, who at his portal firſt
By one deep ſigh a ſign of Life betray'd.

A Maid ſo ſav'd, if but by nature bleſt
With common charms, had ſoon awak'd a flame
More ſtrong than Pity, in that melting heart
Which Pity warm'd before. But ſhe was fair
As Poets picture Hebe, or the Spring;
Graceful withal, as if each limb were caſt

In that ideal mould whence RAPHAEL drew
His Galatea*: Yes, th' impaſſion'd Youth
Felt more than pity when he view'd her charms.
Yet ſhe, (ah, ſtrange to tell) tho' much he lov'd,
Supreſt as much that ſympathetic flame
Which Love like his ſhould kindle: Did he kneel
In rapture at her feet? ſhe bow'd the head,
And coldly bad him riſe; or did he plead,
In terms of pureſt paſſion, for a ſmile?
She gave him but a tear: his manly form,
His virtues, ev'n the courage that preſerv'd
Her life, beſeem'd no ſentiment to wake
Warmer than gratitude; and yet the love
Withheld from him ſhe freely gave his ſcenes;
On all their charms a juſt applauſe beſtow'd;
And, if ſhe e'er was happy, only then
When wand'ring where thoſe charms were moſt diſplay'd.

As thro' a neighb'ring Grove, where antient beech
Their awful foliage flung, ALCANDER led
The penſive maid along, "Tell me," ſhe cry'd,
"Why, on theſe foreſt features all-intent,
"Forbears my friend ſome ſcene diſtinct to give
"To Flora and her fragrance? Well I know

* Ver. 157, Note XXIX.

"That

" That in the general Landſcape's broad expanſe
" Their little blooms are loſt; but here are glades,
" Circled with ſhade, yet pervious to the ſun,
" Where, if enamell'd with their rainbow-hues,
" The eye would catch their ſplendor: turn thy Taſte,
" Ev'n in this graſſy circle where we ſtand,
" To form their plots; there weave a woodbine Bower,
" And call that Bower NERINA's." At the word
ALCANDER ſmil'd; his fancy inſtant form'd
The fragrant ſcene ſhe wiſh'd; and Love, with Art
Uniting, ſoon produc'd the finiſh'd whole.

Down to the South the glade by Nature lean'd;
Art form'd the ſlope ſtill ſofter, opening there
Its foliage, and to each Eteſian gale
Admittance free diſpenſing; thickeſt ſhade
Guarded the reſt.—His taſte will beſt conceive
The new arrangement, whoſe free footſteps, us'd
To foreſt haunts, have pierc'd their opening dells,
Where frequent tufts of ſweetbriar, box, or thorn,
Steal on the green ſward, but admit fair ſpace
For many a moſſy maze to wind between.
So here did Art arrange her flow'ry groups
Irregular, yet not in patches quaint *,

* Ver. 201, Note XXX.

But

But interpos'd between the wand'ring lines
Of ſhaven turf which twiſted to the path,
Gravel or ſand, that in as wild a wave
Stole round the verdant limits of the ſcene;
Leading the Eye to many a ſculptur'd buſt
On ſhapely pedeſtal, of Sage, or Bard,
Bright heirs of fame, who living lov'd the haunts
So fragrant, ſo ſequeſter'd. Many an Urn
There too had place, with votive lay inſcrib'd
To Freedom, Friendſhip, Solitude, or Love.

And now each flow'r that bears tranſplanting change,
Or blooms indigenous, adorn'd the ſcene:
Only NERINA's wiſh, her woodbine bower,
Remain'd to crown the whole. Here, far beyond
That humble wiſh, her Lover's Genius form'd
A glittering Fane, where rare and alien plants
Might ſafely flouriſh *; where the Citron ſweet,
And fragrant Orange, rich in fruit and flowers,
Might hang their ſilver ſtars, their golden globes,
On the ſame odorous ſtem: Yet ſcorning there
The glaſſy penthouſe of ignoble form,
High on Ionic ſhafts he bad it tower
A proud Rotunda; to its ſides conjoin'd

* Ver. 218, Note XXXI.

Two broad Piazzas in theatric curve,
Ending in equal Porticos ſublime.
Glaſs rooft the whole, and ſidelong to the South
'Twixt ev'ry fluted Column, lightly rear'd
Its wall pellucid. All within was day,
Was genial Summer's day, for ſecret ſtoves
Thro' all the pile ſolſtitial warmth convey'd.

These led thro' iſles of Fragrance to the Dome,
Each way in circling quadrant. That bright ſpace
Guarded the ſpicy tribes from Afric's ſhore,
Or Ind, or Araby, Sabæan Plants
Weeping with nard, and balſam. In the midſt
A Statue ſtood, the work of Attic Art;
Its thin light drapery, caſt in fluid folds,
Proclaim'd its antientry; all ſave the head,
Which ſtole (for Love is prone to gentle thefts)
The features of NERINA; yet that head,
So perfect in reſemblance; all its air
So tenderly impaſſion'd; to the trunk,
Which Grecian ſkill had form'd, ſo aptly join'd,
PHIDIAS himſelf might ſeem to have inſpir'd
The chiſſel, brib'd to do the am'rous fraud.
One graceful hand held forth a flow'ry wreath,

The other preſt her zone; while round the baſe
Dolphins, and Triton ſhells, and plants marine
Proclaim'd, that Venus, riſing from the ſea,
Had veil'd in Flora's modeſt veſt her charms.

Such was the Fane, and ſuch the Deity
Who ſeem'd, with ſmile auſpicious, to inhale
That incenſe which a tributary world
From all its regions round her altar breath'd:
And yet, when to the ſhrine ALCANDER led
His living Goddeſs, only with a ſigh,
And ſtarting tear, the ſtatue and the dome
Reluctantly ſhe view'd. And "why," ſhe cry'd,
"Why would my beſt Preſerver here erect,
"With all the fond idolatry of Love,
"A Wretch's image whom his Pride ſhould ſcorn,
"(For ſo his Country bids him)? Drive me hence,
"Tranſport me quick to Gallia's hoſtile ſhore,
"Hoſtile to thee, yet not, alas! to her,
"Who there was meant to ſojourn: there, perchance,
"My Father, wafted by more proſp'rous gales,
"Now mourns his Daughter loſt; my Brother there
"Perhaps now ſooths that venerable age
"He ſhould not ſooth alone. Vain thought! perchance

"Both

" Both periſh'd at Eſopus—do not bluſh,
" It was not thou that lit the ruthleſs flame;
" It was not thou, that, like remorſeleſs Cain,
" Thirſted for Brother's blood: thy heart diſdains
" The ſavage imputation. Reſt thee there,
" And, tho' thou pitieſt, yet forbear to grace,
" A wretched Alien, and a Rebel deem'd,
" With honors ill-beſeeming her to claim.
" My wiſh, thou know'ſt, was humble as my ſtate;
" I only begg'd a little woodbine bower,
" Where I might ſit and weep, while all around
" The lilies and the blue bells hung their heads
" In ſeeming ſympathy." " Does then the ſcene
" Diſpleaſe?" the diſappointed lover cry'd;
" Alas! too much it pleaſes," ſigh'd the fair;
" Too ſtrongly paints the paſſion which ſtern Fate
" Forbids me to return;" " Doſt thou then love
" Some happier youth?" " No, tell thy generous ſoul
" Indeed I do not." More ſhe would have ſaid,
But guſhing grief prevented. From the Fane
Silent he led her; as from Eden's bower
The Sire of Men his weeping Partner led,
Leſs lovely, and leſs innocent than ſhe.

Yet ſtill ALCANDER hop'd what laſt ſhe ſigh'd
Spoke more than gratitude; the War might end;
Her Father might conſent; for that alone
Now ſeem'd the duteous barrier to his bliſs.
Already had he ſent a faithful friend
To learn if France the reverend Exile held:
That friend return'd not. Mean-while ev'ry ſun
Which now (a year elaps'd) diurnal roſe
Beheld her ſtill more penſive; inward Pangs,
From grief's concealment, hourly ſeem'd to force
Health from her cheek, and Quiet from her ſoul.
ALCANDER mourn'd the change, yet ſtill he hop'd;
For Love to Hope his flickering taper lends,
When Reaſon with his ſteady torch retires:
Hence did he try by ever-varying arts,
And ſcenes of novel charm her grief to calm.

Nor did he not employ the Syren Powers
Of Muſic and of Song; or Painting, thine,
Sweet ſource of pure delight! But I record
Thoſe arts alone, which form my ſylvan theme.

At ſtated hours, full oft had he obſerv'd,
She fed with welcome grain the houſehold fowl

That trespaſt on his lawn; this wak'd a wiſh
To give her feather'd fav'rites ſpace of land,
And lake appropriate: in a neighb'ring copſe
He plann'd the ſcene; for there the cryſtal ſpring,
That form'd his river, from a rocky cleft
Firſt bubbling broke to day; and ſpreading there
Slept on its ruſhes. "Here my delving hinds,"
He cry'd, "ſhall ſoon the marſhy ſoil remove,
"And ſpread, in brief extent, a glittering Lake
"Chequer'd with iſles of verdure; on yon Rock
"A ſculptur'd River-God ſhall reſt his urn;
"And thro' that urn the native fountain flow.
"Thy wiſh'd-for bower, Nerina, ſhall adorn
"The ſouthern bank; the downy race, that ſwim
"The lake, or pace the ſhore, with livelier charms,
"Yet no leſs rural, here will meet thy glance,
"Than flowers inanimate." Full ſoon was ſcoopt
The wat'ry bed, and ſoon, by margin green,
And riſing banks, inclos'd; the higheſt gave
Site to a ruſtic fabric, ſhelving deep
Within the thicket, and in front compos'd
Of three unequal arches, lowly all
The ſurer to expel the noontide glare,
Yet yielding liberal inlet to the ſcene;

Woodbine

Woodbine with jaſmine careleſsly entwin'd
Conceal'd the needful maſonry, and hung
In free feſtoons, and veſted all the cell.
Hence did the lake, the iſlands, and the rock,
A living landſcape ſpread; the feather'd fleet,
Led by two mantling ſwans, at ev'ry creek
Now touch'd, and now unmoor'd; now on full ſail,
With pennons ſpread and oary feet they ply'd
Their vagrant voyage; and now, as if becalm'd,
'Tween ſhore and ſhore at anchor ſeem'd to ſleep.
Around thoſe ſhores the Fowl that fear the ſtream
At random rove: hither hot Guinea ſends
Her gadding troop; here midſt his ſpeckled Dames
The pigmy Chanticleer of Bantam winds
His clarion; while, ſupreme in glittering ſtate,
The Peacock ſpreads his rainbow train, with eyes
Of ſapphire bright, irradiate each with gold.
Mean-while from ev'ry ſpray the Ringdoves coo,
The Linnets warble, captive none *, but lur'd
By food to haunt the umbrage: all the Glade
Is Life, is Muſic, Liberty, and Love.

And is there now to Pleaſure or to Uſe
One ſcene devoted in the wide domain

* Ver. 358, Note XXXII.

Its

Its Maſter has not poliſh'd? Rumour ſpreads
Its praiſes far, and many a ſtranger ſtops
With curious eye to cenſure or admire.
To all his Lawns are pervious; oft himſelf
With courteous greeting will the critic hail,
And join him in the circuit. Give we here
(If Candour will with patient ear attend)
The ſocial dialogue ALCANDER held
With one, a youth of mild yet manly mein,
Who ſeem'd to taſte the beauties he ſurvey'd.

"Little, I fear me, will a ſtranger's eye
"Find here to praiſe, where rich Vitruvian Art
"Has rear'd no temples, no triumphal arcs;
"Where no Palladian bridges ſpan the ſtream,
"But all is homebred Fancy." "For that cauſe,
"And chiefly that," the poliſh'd Youth reply'd,
"I view each part with rapture. Ornament,
"When foreign or fantaſtic, never charm'd
"My judgment; here I tread on Britiſh ground;
"With Britiſh annals all I view accords.
"Some Yorkiſt, or Lancaſtrian Baron bold,
"To awe his vaſſals, or to ſtem his foes,
"Yon maſſy bulwark built; on yonder pile,

" In ruin beauteous, I diſtinctly mark
" The ruthleſs traces of ſtern HENRY's hand.

" Yet," cry'd ALCANDER, (interrupting mild
The ſtranger's ſpeech) " if ſo yon antient ſeat,
" Pride of my anceſtors, had mock'd repair,
" And by Proportion's Greek or Roman laws
" That pile had been rebuilt, thou wouldſt not then,
" I truſt, have blam'd, if, there on Doric ſhafts
" A temple roſe; if ſome tall obeliſk
" O'ertopt yon grove, or bold triumphal arch
" Uſurpt my Caſtle's ſtation."—" Spare me yet
" Yon ſolemn Ruin," the quick youth return'd,
" No mould'ring aqueduct, no yawning crypt
" Sepulchral, will conſole me for its fate."

" I mean not that," the Maſter of the ſcene
Reply'd; " tho' claſſic rules to modern piles
" Should give the juſt arrangement, ſhun we here
" By thoſe to form our Ruins; much we own
" They pleaſe, when, by PANINI's pencil drawn,
" Or darkly grav'd by PIRANESI's hand,
" And fitly might ſome Tuſcan garden grace;
" But Time's rude mace has here all Roman piles

" Levell'd

" Levell'd so low, that who, on British ground
" Attempts the task, builds but a splendid lye
" Which mocks historic credence. Hence the cause
" Why Saxon piles or Norman here prevail:
" Form they a rude, 'tis yet an English whole."

" And much I praise thy choice," the stranger cry'd;
" Such chaste selection shames the common mode,
" Which, mingling structures of far distant times,
" Far distant regions, here, perchance, erects
" A fane to Freedom, where her BRUTUS stands
" In act to strike the tyrant; there a Tent,
" With crescent crown'd, with scymitars adorn'd,
" Meet for some BAJAZET; northward we turn,
" And lo! a pigmy Pyramid pretends
" We tread the realms of PHARAOH; quickly thence
" Our southern step presents us heaps of stone
" Rang'd in a DRUID circle. Thus from age
" To age, from clime to clime incessant borne,
" Imagination flounders headlong on,
" Till, like fatigu'd VILLARIO *, soon we find
" We better like a field." " Nicely thy hand
" The childish landscape touches," cries his host,

* Ver. 427, Note XXXIII.

" For Faſhion ever is a wayward child;
" Yet ſure we might forgive Her faults like theſe,
" If but in ſeparate or in ſingle ſcenes
" She thus with Fancy wanton'd: Should I lead
" Thy ſtep, my Friend, (for our accordant taſtes
" Prompt me to give thee that familiar name)
" Behind this ſcreen of Elm, thou there might'ſt find
" I too had idly play'd the truant's part,
" And broke the bounds of judgment." "Lead me there,"
Briſkly the Youth return'd, " for having prov'd
" Thy Epic Genius here, why not peruſe
" Thy lighter Ode or Eclogue?" Smiling thence
ALCANDER led him to the Woodbine bower
Which laſt our Song deſcrib'd, who ſeated there,
In ſilent tranſport view'd the lively ſcene.

" I ſee," his hoſt reſum'd, " my ſportive art
" Finds pardon here; not ev'n yon claſſic form,
" Pouring his liquid treaſures from his vaſe,
" Tho' foreign from the ſoil, provokes thy frown. *
" Try we thy candor farther: higher art,
" And more luxurious, haply too more vain,
" Adorns yon ſouthern coppice." On they paſt
Thro' a wild thicket, till the perfum'd air

* Ver. 448, Note XXXIV.

Gave

Gave to another ſenſe its prelude rich
On what the eye ſhould feaſt. But now the grove
Expands; and now the Roſe, the garden's Queen,
Amidſt her blooming ſubjects' humbler charms,
On ev'ry plot her crimſon pomp diſplays.
"Oh Paradiſe!" the ent'ring youth exclaim'd,
"Groves whoſe rich trees weep odorous gums and balm,
"Others whoſe fruit, burniſh'd with golden rind,
"Hang amiable, Heſperian fables true,
"If true, here only *." Thus, in Milton's phraſe
Sublime, the youth his admiration pour'd,
While paſſing to the dome; his next ſhort ſtep
Unveil'd the central ſtatue: "Heav'ns! juſt Heav'ns,"
He cry'd, "'tis my Nerina." "Thine, mad Youth?
"Forego the word," Alcander ſaid, and paus'd;
His utterance fail'd; a thouſand cluſt'ring thoughts,
And all of blackeſt omen to his peace,
Recoil'd upon his brain, deaden'd all ſenſe,
And at the ſtatue's baſe him headlong caſt,
A lifeleſs load of being.—Ye, whoſe hearts
Are ready at Humanity's ſoft call
To drop the tear, I charge you weep not yet,
But fearfully ſuſpend the burſting woe:

* Ver. 462, Note XXXV.

NERINA's ſelf appears; the further iſle
She, fate-directed, treads. Does ſhe too faint?
Would Heav'n ſhe could! it were a happy ſwoon
Might ſoften her fixt form, more rigid now
Than is her marble ſemblance. One ſtiff hand
Lies leaden on her breaſt; the other rais'd
To heav'n, and half-way clench'd; ſtedfaſt her eyes,
Yet viewleſs; and her lips, which op'd to ſhriek,
Can neither ſhriek nor cloſe. So might ſhe ſtand
For ever: He, whoſe ſight caus'd the dread change,
Tho' now he claſps her in his anxious arm,
Fails to unbend one ſinew of her frame;
'Tis ice; 'tis ſteel. But ſee, ALÇANDER wakes;
And waking, as by magic ſympathy,
NERINA whiſpers, "All is well, my friend;
"'Twas but a viſion; I may yet revive——
"But ſtill his arm ſupports me; aid him, friend,
"And bear me ſwiftly to my woodbine bower;
"For there indeed I wiſh to breathe my laſt."

So ſaying, her cold cheek, and parched brow,
Turn'd to a livid paleneſs; her dim eyes
Sunk in their ſockets; ſharp contraction preſt
Her temples, ears, and noſtrils: ſigns well known

To thoſe that tend the dying *. Both the youths
Perceiv'd the change; and had ſtern Death himſelf
Wav'd his black banner viſual o'er their heads,
It could not more appall. With trembling ſtep,
And ſilent, both convey'd her to the bower.

Her languid limbs there decently compos'd,
She thus her ſpeech reſum'd: "Attend my words
"Brave Cleon! dear Alcander! generous Pair;
"For both have tender intereſt in this heart
"Which ſoon ſhall beat no more. That I am thine
"By a dear Father's juſt commands I own,
"Much-honour'd Cleon! take the hand he gave,
"And with it, Oh, if I could give my heart,
"Thou wert its worthy owner. All I can,
"(And that preſerv'd with chaſteſt fealty)
"Duteous I give thee, Cleon it is thine;
"Not ev'n this dear preſerver, e'er could gain
"More from my ſoul than Friendſhip—that be his;
"Yet let me own, what, dying, ſooths the pang,
"That, had thyſelf and duty ne'er been known,
"He muſt have had my love." She paus'd; and dropt
A ſilent tear; then preſt the ſtranger's hand;

Then

* Ver. 499, Note XXXVI.

Then bow'd her head upon ALCANDER's breaſt,
And "bleſs them both, kind Heav'n!" ſhe pray'd and died.

"And bleſt art thou," cry'd CLEON, (in a voice
Struggling with grief for utterance) bleſt to die
"Ere thou hadſt queſtion'd me, and I perforce
"Had told a tale which muſt have ſent thy ſoul
"In horror from thy boſom. Now it leaves
"A ſmile of peace upon thoſe pallid lips,
"That ſpeaks its parting happy. Go fair ſaint!
"Go to thy palm-crown'd father! thron'd in bliſs,
"And ſeated by his ſide, thou wilt not now
"Deplore the ſavage ſtroke that ſeal'd his doom;
"Go hymn the Fount of Mercy, who, from ill
"Educing good, makes ev'n a death like his,
"A life ſurcharg'd with tender woes like thine,
"The road to Joys eternal. Maid, farewell!
"I leave the caſket that thy virtues held
"To Him whoſe breaſt ſuſtains it; more belov'd,
"Perhaps more worthy, yet not loving more
"Than did thy wretched CLEON." At the word
He bath'd in tears the hand ſhe dying gave,
Return'd it to her ſide, and haſty roſe.
ALCANDER, ſtarting from his trance of grief,

Cry'd " Stay, I charge thee ſtay ;" " and ſhall he ſtay,"
CLEON reply'd, " whoſe preſence ſtabb'd thy peace ?
" Hear this before we part : That breathleſs Maid
" Was daughter to a venerable Sage,
" Whom Boſton, when with peace and ſafety bleſt,
" In rapture heard pour from his hallow'd tongue
" Religion's pureſt dictates. 'Twas my chance,
" In early period of our civil broils,
" To ſave his precious life : And hence the Sire
" Did to my love his Daughter's charms conſign ;
" But, till the war ſhould ceaſe, if ever ceaſe,
" Deferr'd our nuptials. Whither ſhe was ſent
" In ſearch of ſafety, well, I truſt, thou know'ſt ;
" He meant to follow ; but thoſe ruthleſs flames,
" That ſpar'd nor friend nor foe, nor ſex nor age,
" Involv'd the village, where on ſickly couch
" He lay confin'd, and whither he had fled
" Awhile to ſojourn. There (I ſee thee ſhrink)
" Was he that gave NERINA being burnt !
" Burnt by thy Countrymen ! to Aſhes burnt !
" Fraternal hands and chriſtian lit the flame.—
" Oh thou haſt cauſe to ſhudder. I meanwhile
" With his brave ſon a diſtant warfare wag'd ;
" And him, now I have found the prize I ſought,

“ And finding loſt, I haſten to rejoin ;
“ Vengeance and glory call me.” At the word,
Not fiercer does the Tigreſs quit her cave
To ſeize the hinds that robb'd her of her young,
Than he the bower. “ Stay, I conjure thee, ſtay,”
Alcander cry'd, but ere the word was ſpoke
Cleon was ſeen no more. “ Then be it ſo,”
The youth continu'd, claſping to his heart
The beauteous corſe, and ſmiling as he ſpoke,
(Yet ſuch a ſmile as far out-ſorrows tears)
“ Now thou art mine entirely—Now no more
“ Shall duty dare diſturb us—Love alone—
“ But hark ! he comes again—Away vain fear !
“ 'Twas but the fluttering of thy feather'd flock.
“ True to their cuſtom'd hour, behold they troop
“ From iſland, grove, and lake. Ariſe my Love,
“ Extend thy hand—I lift it, but it falls.
“ Hence then, fond fools, and pine ! Nerina's hand
“ Has loſt the power to feed you. Hence and die.”

Thus plaining, to his lips the icy palm
He lifted, and with ardent paſſion kiſt ;
Then cry'd in agony, “ on this dear hand,
“ Once tremblingly alive to Love's ſoft touch,

“ I

"I hop'd to seal my faith:" This thought awak'd
Another sad soliloquy, which they,
Whoe'er have lov'd, will from their hearts supply,
And they who have not will but hear and smile.

And let them smile, but let the scorners learn
There is a solemn luxury in grief
Which they shall never taste; well known to those,
And only those, in Solitude's deep gloom
Who heave the sigh sincerely: Fancy there
Waits the fit moment; and, when Time has calm'd
The first o'erwhelming tempest of their woe,
Piteous she steals upon the mourner's breast
Her precious balm to shed: Oh, it has power,
Has magic power to soften and to sooth,
Thus duly minister'd. ALCANDER felt
The charm, yet not till many a ling'ring moon
Had hung upon her zenith o'er his couch,
And heard his midnight wailings. Does he stray
But near the fated temple, or the bower?
He feels a chilly monitor within,
Who bids him pause. Does he at distance view
His grot? 'tis darken'd with NERINA's storm,
Ev'n at the blaze of noon. Yet there are walks

The loſt one never trod; and there are ſeats
Where he was never happy by her ſide,
And theſe he ſtill can ſigh in. Here at length,
As if by chance, kind Fancy brought her aid,
When wand'ring thro' a grove of ſable yew,
Rais'd by his anceſtors: their Sabbath-path
Led thro' its gloom, what time too dark a ſtole
Was o'er Religion's decent features drawn
By Puritanic zeal. Long had their boughs
Forgot the ſheers; the ſpire, the holy ground
They baniſh'd by their umbrage. "What if here,"
Cry'd the ſweet Soother, in a whiſper ſoft,
"Some open ſpace were form'd, where other ſhades,
"Yet all of ſolemn ſort, Cypreſs and Bay
"Funereal, penſive Birch its languid arms
"That droops, with waving Willows deem'd to weep,
"And ſhiv'ring Aſpens mixt their varied green;
"What if yon trunk, ſhorn of its murky creſt,
"Reveal'd the ſacred Fane?" ALCANDER heard
The Charmer; ev'ry accent ſeem'd his own,
So much they touch'd his heart's ſad uniſon.
"Yes, yes," he cry'd, "Why not behold it all?
"That bough remov'd ſhews me the very vault
"Where my NERINA ſleeps, and where, when Heav'n

"In

" In pity to my plaint the mandate ſeals,
" My duſt with her's ſhall mingle." Now his hinds,
Call'd to the taſk, their willing axes wield;
Joyful to ſee, as witleſs of the cauſe,
Their much-lov'd Lord his ſylvan arts reſume.
And next, within the centre of the gloom,
A ſhed of twiſting roots and living moſs,
With ruſhes thatch'd, with wattled oziers lin'd,
He bids them raiſe *: it ſeem'd a Hermit's cell;
Yet void of hour-glaſs, ſcull, and maple diſh,
Its mimic garniture: ALCANDER's taſte
Diſdains to trick with emblematic toys
The place where He and Melancholy mean
To fix NERINA's buſt, her genuine buſt,
The model of the marble. There he hides,
Cloſe as a Miſer's gold, the ſculptur'd clay;
And but at early morn and lateſt eve
Unlocks the ſimple ſhrine, and heaves a ſigh;
Then does he turn, and thro' the glimm'ring glade
Caſt a long glance upon her houſe of death;
Then views the buſt again, and drops a tear.
Is this idolatry, ye ſage ones ſay? ——
Or, if ye doubt, go view the num'rous train

* Ver. 646, Note XXXVII.

Of poor and fatherlefs his care confoles;
The fight will tell thee, he that dries their tears
Has unfeen angels hov'ring o'er his head,
Who leave their heav'n to fee him fhed his own.

Here clofe we, fweet SIMPLICITY! the tale,—
And with it let us yield to youthful bards
That Dorian reed we but awak'd to voice
When Fancy prompted, and when Leifure fmil'd;
Hopelefs of general praife, and well repaid,
If they of claffic ear, unpall'd by rhyme,
Whom changeful paufe can pleafe, and numbers free,
Accept our fong with candour. They perchance,
Led by the Mufe to folitude and fhade,
May turn that Art we fing to foothing ufe,
At this ill-omen'd hour, when Rapine rides
In titled triumph; when Corruption waves
Her banners broadly in the face of day,
And fhews th' indignant world the hoft of flaves
She turns from Honour's ftandard. Patient there,
Yet not defponding, fhall the fons of Peace
Await the day, when, fmarting with his wrongs,
Old England's Genius wakes; when with him wakes
That plain Integrity, Contempt of gold,

Difdain

Diſdain of ſlav'ry, liberal Awe of rule
Which fixt the rights of People, Peers, and Prince,
And on them founded the majeſtic pile
Of BRITISH FREEDOM; bad fair ALBION riſe
The ſcourge of tyrants; ſovereign of the ſeas;
And arbitreſs of empires. Oh return,
Ye long-loſt train of Virtues! ſwift return
To ſave ('tis ALBION prompts your Poet's prayer)
Her Throne, her Altars, and her laureat Bowers.

THE END.

COMMENTARY

AND

NOTES.

COMMENTARY

ON THE

FIRST BOOK.

GARDENING imparts to rural ſcenery what a noble and graceful deportment confers upon the human Frame: It is not an imitative Art, it is more, it is an endeavour to beſtow on each individual Reality, thoſe beauties which judicious imitation would ſelect from many, and combine in one fictitious Repreſentation. That the Son of Achilles was as much inferior in perſon to his Father, as the moſt perfect human forms are to the fineſt Statues, is the declaration of the ſkilful Philoſtratus; and amounts to a full acknowledgment of the inferiority of individual Nature to ſelective Art. If, therefore, by any means the original can be brought under the obedience of thoſe Laws, by which ſhe is imitated to advantage, an Art is then deviſed as much ſuperior to thoſe which merely deal in imitation, as motion and reality are ſuperior to fiction and inanimate reſt: It is only in right of their conſtitution and laws that the imitative arts are intitled to any preference; but theſe are now transferred and ſet over a more noble dominion. (A)

To eſtabliſh their empire, and pronounce their decrees in the Province of Landſcape, is the purpoſe of the foregoing Poem; to mark the connexion, to point out the principles, and ſometimes to extend the application of the precepts delivered by the Poet, is the purpoſe of this Commentary: it was written originally in the margin of the Poem, and has been ſo fortunate as not only to receive the approbation, but actually now to appear before the world, under the ſanction of its Author. Thus honoured, it is little ſolicitous concerning the reception it may there meet with: For ſhould it even come ſhort of the favourable expectations he has been pleaſed to entertain, and fail to promote the delightful Art it is deſigned to ſerve, one private End, at leaſt, muſt ſtill be anſwered, and my beſt Pride will receive its ample ſatisfaction from ſeeing my name thus publickly connected with that of Mr. Maſon.

From what is here ſaid, it is obvious that the poetical merits of the Engliſh Georgic are not under my conſideration; it will be inferred, perhaps, that I am precluded from giving an opinion on that head; I am ſo: Yet why have I ſtudiouſly conſidered and noted the Poem? The neceſſary anſwer to this queſtion will give

give my judgment; in terms very general, I grant; but thus alone, by leaving it for others to draw the inference, I am enabled to evade the prohibition I am under.

I confeſs that the ſubject alſo, excluſive of the manner in which it has been treated, has charms for me ſufficient to engage my attention: If Reaſon has her Sports, they are worthy the purſuit of Reaſon; and I am far from concurring with the mathematical Reader of Virgil, who, having peruſed the Æneid, laid down the book, and then contemptuouſly pronounced that it might, perhaps, be very good; but for his part he could not ſee the uſe of it, becauſe, forſooth, it proved nothing.

In the claſs with this ſentence we muſt alſo rank the ſurly and ſullen ſpeculation which would inſinuate reflections on an Art that ſucceſsfully undertakes to embelliſh and render Nature univerſally lovely. To extinguiſh the fineſt Faculty of the human Mind, or pervert the natural Taſte for the Pleaſures thence derived, will not, I truſt, however arrogantly claimed, be generally conſidered as the Buſineſs of Reaſon; and therefore we are conſtrained to account for the ſavage and cynical cenſures which would deprive us of the delights of Poetry and Gardening, by referring them to an abſolute ignorance of the reſpective Subjects, and a total defect of the Imagination.

But it is ſo far from being the true Buſineſs of Reaſon to degrade, that to cultivate and enlarge the Imagination is, perchance, the happieſt fruit of her genuine reſearches. It is by means of this ſenſe of the intellect that our convictions, in a thouſand inſtances, become our pleaſures; and by facilitating the comprehenſion of remote objects it is that Reaſon renders them the objects of this Faculty; we are thus rendered ſenſible of the Beauty of Holineſs, the Beauty of Virtue, the Beauty of Syſtem, and even of the Beauty of Theorem; and ſhall an eaſier acceſſibility derogate from our Senſe of the Beauty of Nature? When Reaſon is not diſgraced in thus referring her iſſues to the Imagination, I can ſee no juſt cauſe why our educated ſenſe of Beauty ſhould be ſullenly refuſed the full enjoyment of thoſe objects which, by the benevolent Author of Nature, were originally adapted to her immediate poſſeſſion.

It is not however without ſome diſcriminating powers of the mind that the Beauties of Nature are even diſcerned; the Imagination muſt be correct and pure

pure to ſelect with judgment the ſcenes that are moſt worthy of contemplation. And if to enjoy require an act of the cultivated underſtanding, it will not be denied that to open the ſources of enjoyment, and to deſign and execute, ſo as to give pleaſure to the taſte of an improved intellect, demands the exertion of much greater powers of the mind. What, for example, can be accompliſhed without a critical knowlege of the rules of compoſition, and a vigorous fancy to forecaſt, in each particular inſtance, the future effects of their judicious application? Can a ready obſervation to detect a latent grace, and to diſcern the advantages it is capable of receiving from art, be diſpenſed with? and can the ignorance of any mechanical ſcience be ſuppoſed in the genuine Gardener, whoſe occupation is a perpetual diſplay of even conſummate ſkill in the comprehenſive theories of Painting and Architecture? But, referring my reader to the Author's motto, let me here ceaſe farther to apologize for the liberality of an Art which He, who of all mankind beſt underſtood the true buſineſs of Reaſon, has not diſdained to conſider as "the perfection of civility," or to rank as "the pureſt of human pleaſures."

The Plan of the English Garden is made to correſpond with its ſubject, which is ſingle, and in

which

which the parts, however numerous, are evidently the parts of one uniform whole. The practical precepts, delivered in the three latter Books of the Poem in like manner, are but the amplifications of one fundamental and universally pervading principle, to the doctrine and establishment of which, as a common basis, the commencing book has been accordingly assigned by the Poet.

The Poem begins with an invocation to SIMPLI-
Ver. 1 CITY, the inseparable attendant upon genuine Beauty and Grace; and this with much judgment, because the interference of Simplicity is necessary to control the natural tendency of Art, which is ever more apt to overcharge her work, than fall short of the golden mean, which is the perfection of Nature, and of every artifice to imitate or adorn her. A defective Taste, like a phlegmatic disposition, requires provocatives to excite an interest: Where the Wit of Terence or Addison would fail to obtain a smile, the boisterous and ribbald Jest will be attended by acclamations of joy; and actual afflictions are required to extort a tear from the eye that can view the fictitious miseries of the Stage without emotion. In like manner it is that gaudy hues, violent contrasts, and a surface rough with sculpture and fluttering projections, invite the admira-

tion

tion of ſuch as are blind to the Harmony of colouring, the tender varieties of light and ſhadow, the graces of well-poiſed diſpoſition, and the majeſtic dignity of juſt proportion: And from the ſame principle, it is probable, that the formal magnificence of our antient gardens would, on a compariſon, find a more general ſuffrage than the delicious domeſtic ſcenes which are peculiar to our day: for the ſumptuous Art, which obliterates what it ſhould only adorn, and thus obtrudes itſelf alone upon the eye, ſolicits the vulgar, and will thence obtain a preference to that which, modeſtly miniſtring to Nature, ſets forward only her charms and withdraws itſelf from obſervation. To correct and ſtrengthen the judgment, and conſequently to reform this vicious taſte, is the great purpoſe of the Poet; and while he is about to teach, he ſeeks to place the Conduct of his Poem under the ſame juſt reſtrictions that he preſcribes to the kindred Art which forms its ſubject.—That ſweet Simplicity which ſhould thus preſide in every art, is excellently deſcribed by Quintilian: "Quendam purum, qualis etiam in feminis amatur, "ornatum habet; & ſunt quædam velut é tenui dili-"gentia circa proprietatem ſignificationemque mun-"ditiæ. Alia copiâ locuples, alia floribus læta; vi-"rium non unum genus, nam quicquid in ſuo genere "ſatis effectum eſt valet." *Inſtitut.* lib. viii.

The

Ver. 18 The assistance of the two sister muses of Poetry and Painting, is likewise invoked to promote a kindred Art, an Art in which the attributes of both are engaged: For that Taste which is required either to enjoy, to design, or critically to instruct in the means to design the beauties of scenery, must result from an union of the Poet's delicate feelings, and the Painter's practiced judgment to select the objects by which they are best excited. Ever since the days of Simonides, who declared Painting to be silent Poetry, and Poetry to be speaking Picture, Critics of all ranks and sizes have touched, and some have even extensively expatiated upon the affinity of these two Arts. To prove that Gardening is of their sisterhood, it might be enough to say, that she makes her address to the same mental source of Pleasure, and so rank the whole doctrine under the equally acknowledged assertion of Antiquity, that all the Arts are of one family. Gardening, I grant, has heretofore in a manner withdrawn herself from her relations; for while Nature gave laws to these, and seemed to preside over their friendly society, she alone refused to comply with the dictates which, if possible, more nearly concerned her than the rest. A vigorous imagination, with a correct judgment, were the qualifications which all her sisters sought for in their votaries; while she, with a way-

ward

ward obstinacy, addicted herself to the tasteless Ver.
minions of Fortune, and only required that her woers 18
should be endowed with Wealth. What wonder then that she has been put down from her station, and that her claim to be numbered among the liberal Arts has not been universally acknowledged? But having now become sensible of her own depravity, reformed her errors, and placed herself under the direction of Nature; having lent her whole attention to the laws by which the family is governed; and taken the rules of her present and future conduct from them; her pretensions are no longer problematical: she assumes a dignity that renders her worthy of the rank to which she is restored; has become a favourite in the Train of Nature, the common Mistress of them all; and Painting, who has chiefly taken her under tuition, like the Preceptor of Scipio, declares, that while she imparts, she derives instruction from her ready Pupil.

Having thus, in the poetical mode of invocation, generally intimated the qualifications that are equally requisite in the 'Pupil of his Song' as in the precepts
which teach his Art, after a few episodical lines, upon 25
which, for the reason already assigned, I feel myself with much regret precluded from expatiating, the
Poet, addressing himself to such of the Youth of 30
England, as are enabled by the means of a sufficient

 fortune

Ver. fortune and an unvitiated Tafte of Beauty to carry
his leffons into execution, flides into his fubject
54 with an affurance to fo many of them as are in purfuit
of claffical knowledge, that the Art of Gardening was
61 unknown to antient Rome; and to fuch as vifit the
Continent, that it is not even now to be learned in
63 the detail by travel into modern Italy; but that foreign countries, and particularly that of Italy will,
notwithftanding, contribute natural beauties adapted
to improve or form the tafte, and afford fcenes well
71 worthy of our imitation. Thefe, however, we are
inftructed, not indifcriminately, or too ambitioufly to
83 aim at adopting, for this important reafon, (which
is the firft general precept laid down) that every effort
to improve the fcenery muft correfpond with the
original nature of the place, or elfe moft certainly
prove abortive. (B)

88 But although objects which are inapplicable be
thus profcribed, it does not therefore follow that we
fhould defpair of giving beauty to any fpot however
feemingly defective; for the feeds of grace are univer-
fally diffeminated; and though we cannot any where
raife fuch as are foreign from the foil, and as it were
102 exotic; yet fuch as are indigenous will rife, and attain
107 to their full maturity and perfection under the cultivation

vation of Induſtry and Taſte. The very Heath, for Ver.
example, of all things apparently the leaſt ſuſceptible
of a picturesque appearance, may be fertilized, and
receive a chearful aſpect from the hand of toil;
and taſte ſucceeding to this may carry the work ſo 111
much farther as to beſtow upon it even beauty and
grace: but as the ſoil muſt be reclaimed, in order to
its affording the materials of verdure and foliage to
Taſte, it is evident here that labour muſt go before;
while in the improvement of the dank Vale, which 114
affords another inſtance of their united powers, it is
equally evident that Taſte muſt take the lead, and pre-
cede, or at leaſt conduct the works of labour; for if 123
not, the waters may be drawn off by the ſtraighteſt,
as being the ſhorteſt lines; and theſe again be ſo placed
as to form angular interſections: Whereas Taſte, being at once poſſeſſed of her materials here, will preſcribe that bed or channel in which they may ſpread or run in the moſt beautiful manner; and hence it is that Labour muſt, in this and ſimilar caſes, be the attendant inſtead of the harbinger of Taſte.

And here the valley thus improved is deſcribed; the 129
beauties which Nature has contributed, and the correſponding charms which Fancy has beſtowed, are peculiarized: Time is ſuppoſed to have imparted ma-

Ver. turity to its groves, and ripened all its beauties to the
preciſe idea of the Planter, and it is accordingly found
150 altogether ſuited to contemplation, and the pleaſures
153 of ſecluſion and learned retirement: The cave, the
160 rill, and the ſhadowy glade, adapt it to the Poet; its
copious vegetation, and numerous inſect inhabitants
164 to the Naturaliſt; while, from the general diſpoſition
of its wood and water, and the accidents of light,
which its various parts are formed to catch, the Painter
may derive improvement to his Art. But it is not for
the mere pleaſure of dwelling on the lovely ſcene that
the Poet has thus minutely deſcribed its parts; he had
another view, and has accordingly made his deſcrip-
142 tion the conveyance of an important cenſure on that
indiſcriminating zeal for proſpect which requires and
is only delighted with the extent of unſelected objects;
172 and alſo an exemplification of this doctrine, that a
ſingle ſcene, though not comprehending diſtances,
may yet, by a judicious diſpoſition of light and ſhadow,
be put into poſſeſſion of ſufficient variety to render a
landſcape, thus formed merely of a foreground, complete and perfect within itſelf.

179 If then it appears that Fancy be of ſuch power as
thus to give charms to reluctant Nature, it follows
that we ſhould exert ourſelves to improve this faculty;

and

and to this end it is laid down as a maxim, that we Ver.
ſhould conſult the laws by which Painting is governed,
and apply them to the ſiſter Art of Gardening. But 184
of theſe, the firſt is to make a happy ſelection of objects for the pencil; and therefore, as greatneſs of parts,
a receding gradation of hues and limiting outlines,
and three diſtances, marked each with their reſpective
characters, and bearing to each other a due proportion, are the objects of the Painter's choice, ſo, if 193
they can be attained, they are recommended to the
Gardener as the moſt deſirable ſcenery for the exerciſe
of his imagination and his art.

But of theſe three diſtances, ſuppoſing them poſ- 198
ſeſſed, the foreground is that part which is uſually
moſt at the diſpoſal of a proprietor, and is conſequently
of the higheſt importance. Wherever a Man ſtands
the contiguous objects immediately before him form a
foreground to the ſcene he is looking at; and by the
foreground how much the general proſpect is affected,
there are few who delight in landſcape that have not
perceived. The general harmony of a ſcene reſults
from a due proportion of its parts; but the greater
diſtances are ſeldom within the power of art: How
then ſhall art, thus limited in the extent of her dominion, attempt to harmonize the whole ſcene? To
this

Ver.
this I anſwer, by a judicious adaption and diſpoſition
198 of the objects through which the eye beholds it. A
path is a ſeries of foregrounds; and to adapt each part
of this to the various combinations of the diſtant objects which always reſult from change of place or
aſpect, is the proper buſineſs of art. The effect of
aſpect on a ſcene, and the pleaſure ariſing from an
agreeable ſeries of foregrounds, muſt be ſtrongly felt
by ſuch as ſail upon a fine river between beautiful
banks: by this means we always, as it were, carry
water with us, and render it a permanent ingredient
in a continually changing landſcape. The means then
preſcribed for obtaining a ſimilar permanency in a
beautiful foreground are the direction of the path from
203 which the general ſcenery is to be viewed;—a ſelection of well-adapted greens which ſhall contraſt or
205 mix their colouring into it;—ſuch interruptions as
may frequently give the charm of renewal to what we
207 had been for a time deprived of;—the abſolutely un-
intervening foliage of ſhrubbery beneath the eye;—
209 and the ſhade of foreſt foliage above it; in which
latter caſe the beſt portions of the diſtant ſcene may
be ſelected, and beheld from between the ſtems of the
trees, which ſhould be ſo ſituated as ſometimes by
211 affording lateral limits to reduce the view even to the
ſtricteſt rules of compoſition;—and thus from the va-

rieties

rieties of the foreground the general scene is also perpetually varied.

But as there are many who are not sensible of the 216
beauty of this last feature in a foreground, and hence might too hastily think of removing every forest-tree in front, as only an interruption to the scene, a caution is suggested against such a practice: to prove its necessity, the picturesque principle is resorted to, and exemplified in the wooded foregrounds of Claude Lorrain and G. Poussin; and, as from these it would be impossible to retrench even a single bough without an injury to the general composition of the scene, so Nature is said to suffer a similar injury if her foregrounds are injudiciously deprived of their shade.—
And as, again, the same defective taste which would 225
thus strip the foreground where trees are an important feature, if possessed of power to reach the distances, might there be induced to plant in such a manner as to give them no importance whatever; to counteract the uniform operation of aerial perspective, by spotting the remote hills with little circumscribed clumps of dark foliage; and to intersect by angular fences what is formed to please only by the singleness and majesty of the whole, the picturesque principle, with which the general rules respecting foregrounds are here concluded,

Ver. 225 concluded, is made the means of commencing a new subject, and is accordingly extended to the distant scenes, and in this case exemplified in the distances of Salvator Rosa; for as it would be impossible, among the sublime objects of which these, for the most part, consist, without absolutely subverting the dignity of his whole composition, to introduce the petty contrasts resulting from deep shadowed, but narrowly limited plantations, so Nature is said to suffer a similar injury, if minute inclosures and formal foliage be allowed to disturb the awful tranquility of her more majestic scenes. And the reason is obvious: the whole should be viewed together and not in parts, which would, on account of their remote situation, very distinctly shew their extremities to the eye; whereas in the foreground, neighbourhood intirely precludes the possibility of this effect.

The end and spirit of this precept then being to preserve proportion and harmony in the relative extent and colouring of those parts which enter into the composition of the distant scenery, it will clearly follow that no broad and sober contrasts are precluded by the prohibition. Of nearer objects Nature defines with accuracy at once the outline and the shadow; but losing at a distance the intenseness of both, she

exhibits them with blended and doubtful extremities; Ver.
like twilight she diminishes their opposition, and con- 225
sequently exclaims against whatever should attempt to
give it an unadapted strength: hence dark patches of
ill-consorted wood, which rather seem to stick out
from, than compose a part of, the scene, are her abhorrence. But it is not therefore a woody distance that
is obnoxious either to Her or her Poet; on the contrary, he inculcates this farther doctrine, that extensive
clothing will be productive of the same uniform and
simple greatness as extent of any other character
whatsoever; but he ascertains its manner of application, and instructs us in these cases to give a forest extent of wood to distances even the extremest, and unite
them all by one uninterrupted length of foliage. But
extent and continuity are insisted on as indispensable
here: for as in the sublime ferocity of the scenes, last
considered, no little additions were admitted to interrupt the general union; so where the character of the
distance is forest extent, for the same reason, little in-
termissions are equally precluded. For as clumps and
acute divisions are there said to form a disproportionate 225
contrast, so here the very same defect would result
from formal extremities or circumscribed interruptions
of wood, when opposed to the general hue of the foliage.
And here the particular foliage, by which this great 253

Ver. effect is beſt obtained, is ſpecified, and the Oak, the
253 Elm, and the Cheſnut are recommended to the Planter; their hues are ſufficiently ſimilar, and conſequently that ſpecies of Variety alone, which is naturally incident to diſtances, is aimed at. No fictitious protuberances are affected by the means of paler verdure, nor, altho' the Fir be permitted, as a protection to the other trees, to afford a temporary ſhade, are ſudden, and therefore incongruous, breaks ſought after by the admiſſion of darker greens; the ſcene is left to obtain its variety from the effects of light upon its ſurface; and theſe, let no man doubt, will be ſufficient for his purpoſe: for from the undulating form of this the light and ſhadow will borrow not only extent and breadth, but ſoft and uncertain limits; and even that diverſity of colour which is thus judiciouſly declined by art, will be amply repaid by the ordinary accidents reſulting from the viciſſitudes of weather, and the ſeveral ſeaſons of the day.

264 Thus then we ſee the pictureſque principle exemplified and applied to the living ſcenery of Nature; but we are not for this reaſon to conceive that Nature is thus rendered ſubſervient to an Art over which ſhe has not herſelf previouſly preſided; for, tho' ſhe may not in every portion of her works have exhibited the full perfection

perfection of beauty, yet in ſome ſhe probably has; Ver.
and though, wherever theſe lovely features occur, ſhe 264
may not in every inſtance have combined them to the
greateſt poſſible advantage; yet in ſome ſhe has certainly diſplayed the charms of harmonious compoſition.
Had ſhe done this univerſally, or where ſhe has done
it, were it the talent of every man to obſerve and to
generalize the principle on which ſhe has proceeded,
it would be unneceſſary here to call in the aid of an
imitative Art; but when to thoſe alone who have 280
cultivated this, the ſkill to ſelect and recombine the
beauties of Nature, has been heretofore in a manner
confined, to thoſe it cannot be deemed unreaſonable
to refer the Gardener for inſtruction in the conduct of
his own art. To grace and adorn the perſon of the
great original herſelf is his pleaſing province; and
ſurely He is the moſt likely to ſucceed in the diſcharge
of this duty, who moſt diligently inveſtigates the principles on which ſhe has already been imitated with
the happieſt ſucceſs. From thoſe then who, with the
higheſt Taſte and moſt diſcriminating powers of ſelection, have transferred the beauties of Nature to the
canvas, we may, without derogation, ſubmit to receive inſtruction, and learn ourſelves to ſelect, to digeſt,
and to diſpoſe our ſuperiour materials, according to

Ver. rules of composition that have been primarily dictated
280 by herself.

300 It is not, therefore, by declining the study of Nature, that we are desired to aim at attaining that abstract Idea of Beauty to which we should for ever refer our designs and works, but by studying her through the medium of an Art which, upon her own principles, has combined and improved her features; thus we are ascertained of success, and having once got possession of this general archetype, we see every species of littleness fly before it; every symptom of mechanism withdraws, and every trace of geometric
312 order is obliterated; the Angle declines into the waving Curve, and parts, before acutely divided, now melt into each other with soft and easy transitions.

318 And such a transition the Poet may be said to have here exemplified in his own method. We had before been instructed how far the Powers of Fancy were able to contend with the difficulties started by Nature herself, and to remove what appeared to be even deformity; and now from a general rule, in which his abhorrence of mechanick order is inculcated, we are carried to the consideration of her equal powers to reform the absurdities introduced by antecedent

Art.

Art. The right lined Viſta conſequently, however ſanctified by time or circumſtance, is condemned to fall, while only ſuch of its trees as can ſurvive removal, or ſuch as, by concealment of their line, may plead for mercy, can hope to avert the ſtroke of the Axe: from theſe few, however, a conſiderable effect is promiſed; and thus Art, in concurrence with Nature, and acting only as her handmaid, is ſeen reſtoring to Beauty Scenes, which, without that concurrence, ſhe had herſelf previouſly deformed. (C)

We have now ſeen the pictureſque principle eſtabliſhed, and we have traced its operations in the improvement of defective Nature, and the reformation of erroneous Art. We have ſeen it alſo more agreeably occupied in ſelecting, heightening, and arranging the Features of an extenſive Landſcape originally beautiful: we are now to contemplate its effect upon the only ſpecies of rural view that has not yet been brought under its direction: But in this inſtance the precept is Caution; and ſo very tenderly is Art permitted to touch the almoſt-finiſhed work of Nature, that its interference ſeems rather to be prohibited than invited here. If indeed the ſcene fall ſhort of the Poet's deſcription, and yet conſiſt of parts that are capable of being rendered conformable to it, it is

then

Ver. then the delightful office of Art to break new ground,
and for the firſt time to enter into the ſhadowy wild,
348 which bears no mark of ever having heretofore been
invaded by the hand of man: but here good Taſte
will hold ſacred the deep ſolemnity, the ſilent and
ſolitary grandeur of its dark receſſes; it will move on
without impreſſing a diſtinguiſhable veſtige, and will
only, as it were, by ſtealth admit the human eye to
355 the enjoyment of their ſecluded beauties. If Time indeed, giving to oblivion every unpleaſing idea of
their former deſignation, has handed over to Nature,
and ſhe adopting them has blended with her own
360 offspring the antient ſeats of tyranny and ſuperſtition,
Fancy has little more to do than to enjoy the vale,
whoſe woody ſides, forming a gloomy contraſt to the
rocks that glitter through them, are over-hung by
the majeſtick Ruins of a Caſtle; or in the bottom of
perhaps the ſame valley to contemplate the more awful Remains of an Abbey ſtanding on the margin of a
ſtream, by which the whole is watered: For what indeed remains for her to do? If abſolute neglect has
obſcured the beauties of the ſcene, or rendered it, perhaps, inacceſſible, an acceſs muſt be obtained, and
its beauties muſt be retrieved from a circumſtance
equivalent to annihilation: but this is the utmoſt that
is allowed to Art, and even in the performance of
theſe

theſe neceſſary offices, the principal attention muſt be Ver.
paid to the concealment and diſguiſe of its inter- 360
ference. Hence the Poet, inſtead of imparting his inſtruction in this inſtance in the form of precept, has conveyed it by a deſcription, and finding ſo little matter for maxim, inſtead of a leſſon, has given us an archetype for our imitation.

From the contemplation of Scenes like theſe, the 386
Poet now ſuddenly directs our obſervation to the geometrical abſurdities of our antient Gardens, and by thus artfully bringing them into immediate compariſon, excites our juſt indignation againſt their unnatural and ſumptuous puerilities: Our eye, but now in the enjoyment of Nature's lovelieſt freeſt forms, beholds, with diſguſt, the narrow reſtraints under which ſhe has heretofore been oppreſſed. Where Art takes Nature for its Archetype, Nature may herſelf improve under the conduct of that Art; but where on the contrary its ſource is in itſelf, or to be found rather in the principles than the viſible performances of Nature, the works of Art like this, are never to be adopted in her domains. Painting preſents a mirrour to her form; and before this ſhe may dreſs herſelf to the improvement of her charms: but what can Architecture contribute to heighten them? Having ne-

ver

Ver. ver borrowed from her it has nothing to restore; and
386 to become a borrower herself, is a condescension beneath the dignity of her character; and consequently, however graceful, however majestick the works of this fine Art may rise, their beauties are their own, they are peculiar to themselves, and in no respect applicable to the forms of Nature, who will therefore
392 scorn to wear them. Boundless in her easy variety she disdains the restrictions of the line and plummet, and, that substitute for the chizzel, the sheers. Yet such were the antient implements of the Gardener; by these the green Arcade was formed, and the dwarf vegetable trimmed into the mosaic pavement of the parterre; by these its angular extremities and quick, smooth slope were given to the terras: by these the winding currents of water were compelled to stagnate in straight canals; and, to use the language of an old French Writer, by these they were effectually prevented from ever degenerating into Rivers again.

The History of Gardening in England, from the days of Elizabeth to our own time, finds here an easy introduction, it is accordingly related, and hence we learn the antiquity of that formal mode which has just been condemned; we also learn that however

obstinately it held its ground, it had yet in every age
come under the censure of the wisest and most dis- Ver.
cerning men; that yielding at last to their remon- 498
strances and ridicule, it began to give way about the commencement of the present century; and, consequently, that at that period the style which forms the subject of the Poem may be said to have had its rise, although it has but very lately attained to its
perfection. To the works of those great Masters, 536
therefore, who have brought it to this high state, as before to the works of the Painter, we are now referred, with an earnest assurance, that by them we shall see the principles of the Art exemplified, and from the study of their practice, be enabled to correct our Taste and extend our Fancy; that by exercising these, and giving an actual existence to whatever ideal forms and combinations we may have derived from all the sources that have now been laid open to us, we may bestow beauty upon even the ordinary features of natural scenery, and enter into the refined enjoyment of whatever Nature has, in this kind, created most lovely and complete. (D)

Having now brought the Commentary on the First Book to a conclusion, and throughout endeavoured to maintain and strengthen the great principle of rural beauty which has been preſcribed by the Poet, I ſeem to hear an objection ſtarted to the juſtice of the doctrine, and to be aſked in what manner the practice of the Gardener, who, for the moſt part, makes exceſſive neatneſs an object in his ſcenes, is to be reconciled with that ſpecies of beauty which conſiſts in roughneſs of ſurface, and which appears to have been always aimed at by the Painter of Landſcape.

To this, in the firſt place, I anſwer, that the objection does not affect the general compoſition, which is ſtill moulded according to the pictureſque idea; and, ſecondly, that it cannot affect the diſtances, which are beyond the reach of any ſuch ſubordinate conſideration. How far then does it extend? Only to the foreground; and even in this, not to the deſign, but the pencilling; for, excluſive of the ſurface, the form may be preſerved to the moſt faſtidious expectations of the Painter. What then remains? not the drawing of the Picture, for that is allowed to be correct, but juſt the manner of handling that ſmall domeſtic portion which lies immediately beneath the eye. And, ſurely, when it comes to be conſidered, that in generalizing a principle, and applying it to a new ſubject, ſome variety muſt always reſult from the application; and this not from any mutability of the principle itſelf, but from the

the diverſity of the objects with which it is combined, a variety ſo extremely trivial, can hardly be admitted as an objection to the introduction of the pictureſque principle into the Art of Gardening; it falls before this ſelf-evident propoſition, that a rural ſcene in reality, and a rural ſcene upon canvas, are not preciſely one and the ſame thing.

But that point, in which they differ here, is not itſelf without a guiding principle: Utility ſets up her claim, and declares, that however concurrent the genuine Beauty of Nature and Picture may be, the Garden Scene is hers, and muſt be rendered conformable to the purpoſes of human life; if to theſe every conſonant charm of painting be added, ſhe is pleaſed; but by no means ſatisfied, if that which is convertible to uſe be given abſolutely to wildneſs. The Wildneſs of Nature, therefore, is irretrievably ſet aſide, and, conſequently, it is only that kind of beauty which wears the ſtamp of human interference that can be cultivated here. Admit that deſart Nature is beſt arrayed in the rough garb which painting chuſes to imitate; yet in the Engliſh Garden, even in her very fineſt ſcenery, it is not deſirable to preſerve her in ſuch a ſtate of uſeleſs purity, that it ſhall appear as if no human footſtep had even trod the ground. The

 preſence

presence of the mansion must for ever refute the supposition. Neatness must, consequently, supersede this savage air, for meer slovenly accommodation is, of all defects, the most disgusting, it is a mean between wildness and cultivation, which makes each destructive of the other, and, consequently, instead of being both, is really neither. To neatness, therefore, the surface of the foreground must be given: the claims of utility must be complied with, for the rudeness of Nature is precluded, and this alone remains: but even from this no small share of picturesque beauty may be made to arise, and smoothness itself, if thus the means and reasons of creating it appear, and that the shaven Lawn be seen covered with the flocks which have been the instruments of its polish, will be found in a very extensive degree to conform to the principle originally prescribed. But I will now go even further, and aver, that it altogether conforms: The Arts which imitate Nature are necessarily defective in one point, they cannot imitate her motion; and hence they are driven to seek for some substitute that may be productive of the same effect. A roughness of surface is produced by quick contrasts of contiguous Light and Shade, which resulting in the appearance of frequent projection and retirement, the Eye, by the rapid succession of these, is affected in exactly the ſame manner as if the parts were actually moving before it: But is this roughneſs, therefore, neceſſary in Nature herſelf? It certainly is not; and the reaſon is, that poſſeſſing a real, it would be ſuperfluous to adopt the means by which only a fictitious motion is atchieved: the PRINCIPLES of Painting, therefore, are univerſally received; and thus THE ENGLISH GARDEN, exempted from the neceſſity of uſing them, is found only not to accept of the artificial reſources of Picture.

COMMENTARY

ON THE

SECOND BOOK.

THE Poet having, in the former Book, propofed every general principle relating to the Art of Gardening, it would have been allowable for him to have laid down his pen, and left his readers, in each particular inftance, to have made the application as well as they could for themfelves: But reflecting on the difficulty of carrying general theories into practice, he has himfelf condefcended to take his Pupil by the hand, and to teach him to apply his rules in every portion of his fubject. He enters accordingly in the following Books into the detail, and inftructs us in the means of executing every part of that great whole with which we had been previoufly made acquainted; we have feen the Picture; we have admired the Compofition; and even contemplated its greater features; but we are now to imitate it; we muft, therefore, defcend to fubordinate confiderations; we are no longer to confider the effect alone, but to enquire into the means by which it is produced; and to the fpeculative part of Gardening, henceforward learn to afford the affiftance of manual operation.

The

Ver. The regard that is due to Utility, and the neceſſity
which ſubſiſts of rendering even Beauty no more than
an adjunct to this in the Engliſh Garden, has been
already intimated: to ſome reflections on the happy
effects of their union the preſent portion of the ſubject
now naturally leads the mind; and, accordingly, the
1 Second Book opens with an Addreſs to an Art which
thus benevolently turns Magnificence from the cultivation of ſumptuous trifles to the improvement of that
which is beneficial to mankind. But here, while we
18 attend to the precept conveyed in this apoſtrophe, we
muſt be exceedingly on our guard not to miſapply it,
or imagine, that by converting beautiful objects to
any other than their appropriate uſe, we are acting
under its direction: The genuine ſpirit and tendency
of the rule is not to turn ornament to uſe; it is the
converſe of this, and inſtructs us only to make utility
the ſubject of ornament (E). But even this law is
not without its liberal conſtruction: in the great it
muſt, perhaps, be literally interpreted; yet, like Poetry, Gardening will frequently acquieſce in a fiction
of utility, accept of an End for a Uſe, and ſtamp the
means which effect it, and the juſt adaption of the
ornaments to the ſeeming purpoſe, with the name
and characters of Truth.

Under

Under the authority of this general maxim then, it Ver.
is obvious that the antient formal ſtyle of Gardening 35
muſt neceſſarily fall: the Gardener will endeavour to
reſtore to Nature whatever ſhe has been ſo long deprived of: but as in the infancy of his art there is
danger, that in deſtroying the right-lined diſpoſition of
his ground, he ſhould, as was really the fact, run into 47
the oppoſite extreme, a caution is ſuggeſted againſt all
exceſſive and overſtrained curvatures, and that eaſy 51
line, which is a mean between them, and which is
ſpontaneouſly traced in the pathway of every Being 56
that moves under the unaffected direction of Nature,
is deſcribed as the only legitimate ſource of beauty
and genuine grace; of this ſoft and melting curve the
application, we are told, muſt be univerſal; and that 71
not only the pathway, and the outline of wood and water muſt be guided by it, but that the form of the ſurface of the ground itſelf muſt come under its direction.

But however gracefully it may flow, and however
conſidered in itſelf, it may appear to be an abſolute
ſtranger to geometric rules, yet as all paralleliſms 82
muſt thence derive their ſource, even this curve muſt not be matched with its own parallel: the green-ſward, therefore, through which the pathway winds, muſt be varied in its breadth, and the neighbouring

Ver. objects ſtand at that variety of diſtance that con-
86 traſt may reſult; in like manner the ſurface of the
90 ground ſhould be diverſified in its form; and in every
inſtance, whether of hill, ground-plan, or plantation,
the idea of pairs muſt be diligently avoided. Without this equality the balance may be ſufficiently main-
92 tained, and the means of preſerving it are preſcribed
by Nature herſelf; it is not by copying one feature
from another that ſhe proceeds to create a harmony of
parts, ſhe accompliſhes this end with more variety,
nor finds it even neceſſary to place her correſpondencies
at an equal diſtance from the point of view; for to the
remote Mountain ſhe frequently oppoſes the neighbouring Shade or Rock, and thus ſatisfies the expectations of the Eye with difference and uniformity
at once. Hence then Art ſhould derive its rule, and
by a like oppoſition of diſſimilar objects give poize
and regularity to the general Compoſition of her
105 Works: the Foreground is her proper diſtrict, here
therefore every object, whether of ſurface or plantation, may be formed according to the Taſte of the
Proprietor; their mutual adaption is, conſequently,
at his diſpoſal, and he is accordingly inſtructed in the
manner of ſuiting both their forms and hues, not only
to each other, but to the diſtant ſcenery which is beheld from among them.

But

But in this, and every other operation of Art, the Ve
particular character of the scene must be most atten- 110
tively considered, and cultivation assume a manner
from the subject with which it connected; thus the
introduction of soil, sufficient to maintain the vegetation of forest trees among the rocky clefts, may prove 126
the means of removing the black and desolated Air of
a Scene, whose proper character is Majesty; and thus
by a junction of Wood and Rock, and thence a happy
contrast of gloom and glitter, Dignity may be made to
supersede a cold and forbidding aspect. The swelling 139
Hillock may be made to vary the fatiguing sameness
of the Flat, while this again, opposed by Plantations,
may result in an animated and chearful Landscape;
and in like manner variety may be introduced into the 145
very Thicket, its uniform darkness may be chequered
by clearing away the inferiour wood, while the re-
maining Shade will borrow dignity from the contrast-
ed Light that is thus admitted into it; the rivulet too 152
should here be allowed to sparkle in the sun and assist
the opposition; and thus we see not only the balance
well adjusted, but the cure that may, by attention to
its genius, be applied to the defects of each particular
species of scenery.

But of all the purposes on which the character of a 159
Scene should be consulted, that is the most important

Ver. which determines the mode of adapting ornament to
159 Use, without permitting it to encroach upon the
limits by which it should be restricted; of these, as
we have already observed, it is the business of the
gardener to make such a Union, that neither may
& prove injurious to the other; ornament must not in-
fringe the claims of Utility, while, at the same
time, it is essential that Utility should not sordidly
reject the ornament with which it is becomingly arrayed. But it is a Truth, which experience will
161 speedily evince, that nothing is more difficult than to
preserve the proper boundary of these; Pleasure in its
wantonness would seek to appropriate what should
be destined to more profitable purposes; and there is
hardly to be found a profitable Purpose to which
ground may be turned, that is not likely to invade
the equitable claims of Pleasure; the very sheep, in
their browzing, thus destroy the bloom and foliage
which give beauty to the Pathway that steals round
their pasture. Where then is the remedy to be
167 found? in the Fence, alone; we must ascertain their respective Limits; we must divide and yet not disunite,
and the expedient is as practicable as it is necessary;
the Fence, by winding freely, may for ever be with-
170 drawn from the eye, and the very foliage, which it
serves to protect, will at every bend conceal it from
the

the view. The form of the ground, in each particular instance, will instruct in some peculiar means 170
of disguising the division, but in all it should
be drawn with that bold line, that the trees and 178
shrubbery which adorn the pathway, should frequently project into, and appear to blend themselves with the field; while the field, in like manner, should frequently be seen to form recesses among these projected trees; and here, when the sheep go into these, they will seem to be uncontrolled, and the only evidence to the contrary will afterwards be, that nothing has been destroyed.

Having thus far spoken of the Fence, as the neces- 245
sity for its concealment, and the general form of its line are concerned, the Poem now enters into a more practical discussion of the various kinds that may be resorted to, and the properest means to render them at once effectual and invisible; and of these, the first that is recommended to our choice, is that which
is commonly known by the name of the Sunk Fence; 260
by this the ground which is seen beyond it, provided its manner of cultivation be any thing similar, appears so intimately and continuously united with that on which we stand ourselves, that it is almost always with surprize the division is discovered; and hence,

Ver. hence, as expressive of that passion, it obtained, when
260 first invented, the name of the Ha! Ha! The mode of
constructing this is specified, and is as follows: Dig
265 deep a trench, and to the base of the side from which
you look, and which must be perpendicular and fronted
with stone, the opposite side must be gently sloped
from the level of the soil; the verdure of this slope
must be preserved, and the wall which sustains the
272 neighbouring side, must be covered on its top also with
the green turf, a little raised above the surface of the
soil. This is the strongest manner of constructing the
Sunk Fence; but the greatest strength is not in every
instance necessary; it may, indeed, be requisite, in
284 order to restrain the Deer, but cattle of a tamer kind,
will be turned without it; the perpendicularity and
the stone front of the nearer bank may, therefore, be
288 here dispensed with, and in their place a slope, and
at midway down a row of thorns, defended when
young with pointed pales, may be substituted; but
this must be kept from surmounting the level of the
300 Lawn, and its surface made always parallel to the
bank on which it grows.

305 But the form of the surface of the ground, the direction in which it is to run, and the nature of the
inconvenience to be excluded, must, in every particular case, determine the sort of Fence that should be

made

made use of; that which we have already seen is best Ver.
applied, when its line runs directly across the Eye, 306
for in this instance it becomes absolutely invisible;
but on the contrary it becomes, of all deformities, 308
itself the most disgusting, if ascending the Hill in
front, or in any other manner offering its end to the
view, it exhibits only a gaping interruption of the
otherwise continuous surface: in these cases, therefore, we must have recourse to new expedients, and
if sheep only are to be excluded from the Pathway,
a sufficient defence against their inroads may be obtained from net-work, or wire extended upon com- 319
mon stakes; three rows of stronger cordage stretched
between posts must be opposed to horses and oxen (F);
but as these are all liable to a thousand injuries and 330
a swift decay, and consequently will require a trouble-
some degree of attention to keep them in repair, a 336
more durable substitute, but chiefly where the division
is at some little distance, is allowed of, and for this 350
purpose a well-constructed paling of wood-work is
recommended; but as this again might very probably obtrude itself upon the Eye, while it is not
possible that a fence of any kind can be an ornament, we are instructed in the best means of miti-
gating the necessary evil, and preventing its becoming
a defect.

The

The means then are briefly theſe; give to your
362 paling no tawdry glare, but as near as poſſible the
colour of the ground againſt which it is ſeen; for thus
the Eye ſhall blend them together, and thus the
ground in a manner ſhall abſorb the Fence. And
here the poet, ſtrongly feeling, and wiſhing to inculcate,
the neceſſity of this precept, is exceedingly particular,
and has left it only for me to reduce his farther inſtruc-
tions on this head, to the form of a recipe, in
which, however, I am obliged to omit the quantity of
each ingredient, becauſe it muſt always depend upon
the circumſtances of the ſcenery in which the paint
367 is made uſe of; take then White-Lead, Oker, Blue-
Black, and a proportionably ſmall quantity of Verdi-
greaſe, and making of theſe an oil paint, ſpread it on
393 the paling; the effect of this, if uſed with judge-
ment, will be found fully anſwerable to the moſt
ſanguine expectations; the limits, as it were, retire
from the view, and Uſe and Beauty, which ſeemed
to have ſuffered a momentary divorce, are now indiſ-
tinguiſhably united again.

407 But there is a Fence of which the concealment is
not equally neceſſary, a Fence which genuine taſte
will even rejoice to contemplate, for of genuine taſte
humanity is the inſeparable aſſociate; on the children,

therefore,

therefore, of the labouring Peasants, we are previ- *Ver.*
ously desired to confer the charge of superintending all 407
our boundaries, and guarding them from the invasions of herds and flocks; in order to adapt them to
this little stewardship, to change their weeds of 430
poverty for a more cleanly and comfortable attire; and arming the infant shepherds with the proper implements of their picturesque office, to employ and post them where they may be even conspicuously seen.

From this benevolent precept, the Poet is naturally 460
led to consider the blessings and mental improvements which attend upon the active occupations and the contemplative retirement of the Gardener, and concludes the book with an Episode in which they are eminently illustrated. The scenery of the piece is well deserving of our attentive observation, and the sentiment, however poetically blazoned, stands firm upon the basis of historic evidence.

Cicero has spoken of retirement in terms not very different from those which introduce the Tale of Abdalonimus: "Quis enim hoc non dederit nobis, "ut cum operâ nostrâ Patria sive non possit uti, sive "nolit, ad eam vitam revertamur, quam multi docti

Ver. "homines, fortasse non recte, sed tamen multi etiam
460 "reipublicæ præponendam putaverunt." *Cic. Epist.* *lib.* ix. *epist.* vi. But, surely, the Poet has spoken more decisively like a patriot than even this great deliverer of his country himself; he has not preferred secession to the cause of the public; on the contrary, he has described it as a means of cultivating every talent for its service, and a sort of watch-tower from which to look out for the happy moment when they may be called into action; and in the conduct of his Hero, has presented it to us in the light of a school, in which the lessons of magnanimity and moderation are taught; and in which the well-disposed mind, abstracted from the pursuits of the world, will learn the duty of foregoing every private indulgence when the sacrifice may render us the fortunate instruments of restoring prosperity to our country, or extending the happiness of our species.

I do not exclusively challenge for Gardening the whole of those attributes which have been by a thousand writers ascribed to Agriculture at large, any more than I should exclusively claim to the most perfect knowledge of architectural ordonnance the entire eulogy that might be pronounced on the art of constructing habitations. Without the stately column or fretted

fretted roof the Savage might receive protection from the ſtorm, and without the picturеſque ſcene the nerves of labour might be braced, and the markets ſupplied with the ordinary productions of the field: But on the other hand, without ſome portion of theſe refinements, are Agriculture and Architecture adapted to the exerciſe or reception of an Engliſh Gentleman? Certainly they are not; and yet, as we are now inſtructed to diſpoſe the Garden-ſcene, the occupations of the Farm are not excluded from it; the purpoſes of life are not only attended to, but conſulted. Magnificence is no longer a Tyrant, deriving his honours from the deſolation of his territories; aſſuming a milder royalty, he now ſeeks his chief glory from their fertile ſtate; he ſets his poliſh upon accommodation, and it is henceforward Utility that the King delighteth to honour. What, therefore, can now be ſaid in the praiſe of Agriculture that may not be extended to Gardening, with this additional felicity, that being endowed with Pleaſures of its own, it counteracts the guilty temptations of faſhionable Vice, and renders the favourites of Fortune partakers with the peaſant in the bleſſings of innocency and health, without, at the ſame time, impoſing upon them the neceſſity of ſharing in his toil; enjoying at once the opportunities of ſalubrious exerciſe and contemplative leiſure, unaffected by the little cares of the world, and unalienated by feeing their unamiable influence upon others, exempt, fo far as human nature can be exempt, from the affaults of irretrievable difappointment, Contentment, which generates the love of man, and a fenfe of gratitude which, if not the thing itfelf, muft neceffarily refult in the Love of God, take poffeffion of their hearts, and affume the conduct of their virtuous lives; and hence, with the man who tills his own ground, the Gardener may be juftly characterized as "one who inflicts no terror; who entertains no hoftile difpofition, but is an univerfal friend; whofe hands, unftained with blood, are devoutly confecrated to that God who bleffes his orchards, his vintage, his threfhing-floor, and his plough; who vindicates his equality in an equal ftate, and ftrenuoufly oppofes himfelf to the unconftitutional encroachments of Ariftocratic or Monarchic Power." (G)

COM-

COMMENTARY

ON THE

THIRD BOOK.

IN an apoſtrophe to his memory, the Poet now introduces his late lamented friend, Mr. Gray, as delivering his opinion on the ſubject of the preſent Poem, and declaring the preference which he gave to the works of Nature over every effort of Art. We are not, however, to conceive that he condemned her juſt exertions, becauſe he prefers the more majeſtic ſublimity of Nature; the contrary inference will follow from the precept with which he cloſes his animated counſel: for after he has ſhowed the inferiority of art's creative powers, he yet proceeds to regulate her conduct, and ſtating her proper office, adviſes her to conform to the Canon of Nature, and only to curb every fantaſtic or capricious variation from her great example. (H)

The ſubject of the Engliſh Garden is not, like that of Thomſon's Seaſons, a mere deſcriptive Eulogy on the luxuriances and beauties of Nature; it is preceptive, and its end is to poliſh Huſbandry, and inſtruct

ſtruct us in the art of preſerving thoſe very beauties as far as may be reconcilable with the neceſſities of cultivation: theſe had, in the antient mode of Gardening, been altogether ſuperſeded; to teach the means, therefore, of recalling them is, ſurely, not ſetting up Art as a rival to Nature, it is making it ſubſervient and contributary to her ends. If the rude magnificence of untouched Nature could conſiſt with appropriation, it would be unneceſſary to preſcribe any rule; but when we know that it cannot, and that heretofore a falſe idea of beauty has been entertained, ſhall we, therefore, depreciate the value of the leſſon that conveys a better? Or ſhall we, becauſe the praiſe of Nature is higher than that of Art, declare that Art is not deſerving of our attention? The argument, that on this ground would militate againſt the Engliſh Garden, will be found to go a great deal farther, and extend to the ſubverſion of every other imitative art as well as the Art of Gardening.

As we have all along conſidered the Garden as a Picture, ſo we are under the neceſſity of conſidering the unadorned and naked ſoil as the Painter's canvas, and, conſequently, of looking on every means of ornament as the pencils and colours with which he is to work. But the canvas, with the coarſe outlines of the

the scene, are supplied by Nature; the former Book Ver.
has corrected the drawing; and now we come to give
it all the variety of tints that Wood and Water can
afford; from these it is true the landscape will derive
its most important charms of light and shadow, they
are nevertheless represented only in the light of super-
added, though natural, ornaments, as not being essential to the existence of the scene which, considered
in this light, we see may subsist without them. From 63
the conduct of the Pathway, the Fence, and the
Ground-plan, therefore, the subject now changes
first to the proper disposition of Wood; and the picturesque purposes of planting being to conceal deformities and create ornament, the Planter, tho' it is
declared unnecessary for him to be an adept in all 87
the science of the Naturalist, with respect to the classi-
fication of trees, is yet required skilfully to know their 96
several forms, their sizes, their colours, their manner
of growing, and other external characters, in order
that he may be always able to apply them respectively
to those purposes which they are best adapted to answer; for his ignorance of these may lead him into
bad mistakes; the Pine, for instance, by its quick 108
growth and branching arms, seems well calculated to
shut out the low wall or fence from the view, yet a
better acquaintance with its habits, will shew its un-

fitness;

Ver. fitneſs; for as it riſes it is found to ſhake off thoſe
115 very arms that might ſerve to tempt the planter to uſe
it. Box, therefore, and Holly, &c. are declared more
eligible here, becauſe they are found to thicken below, and being planted not for their own beauty,
but to hide what is defective in other objects, may be
brought by the pruning knife to any form that moſt
118 effectually promotes this end. But above all plants,
the Laurel has received a preference from the Poet, as
at once both anſwering this purpoſe, and being in
136 itſelf alſo poſitively beautiful. With theſe evergreens,
it is farther recommended to blend ſuch indigenous
ſhrubs as are of early bloom, and though the utmoſt
150 nicety of ſelection be not attended to, yet we are
promiſed a good general effect, one rule only being
153 obſerved, which is to range the darker foliage behind
as a ground to fling forward that which has a brighter
hue, and, in Autumn, by their undecaying verdure, to
give brilliancy to the ruſſet colour which is acquired
by the dying deciduous leaves; but this latter reaſon
161 is not inſiſted on, the Spring and Summer being
deemed of more important conſideration: in order,
163 however, to prevent any breach in the ſkreen from the
decay of leaves in Winter, the greateſt care muſt be
taken to preſerve the line of Evergreens entire.

Such

Such is the remedy for low deformities, but to ex- Ver.
clude those of loftier stature, the intervention of forest- 169
trees, so planted as not to overhang the underwood-shrubbery, is required; and these may be so managed, as that while they conceal a part they may, at the same time, convert the remainder of a structure even to an ornamental object. When the barn-like choir and chancel of a country Church, for instance, are by means of such a skreen as this shut out from the view, what can afford a more pleasing appearance than the tower which remains among the deep-shadowing foliage that has served to conceal them?

It only now remains to consider planting in the 185
light of ornament, and as it serves at once to harmonize, and give energy to that opposition of light and shade which results, perhaps, too tenderly from the easy surface of the soil. To the general maxims delivered in the first book upon this subject, the following more particular precepts are therefore now added, and taken together, the whole may be considered as a complete code of all the laws that relate to this subject.

Where the ground is so elevated as to be itself an 195
obstruction, the interposition of foliage cannot any

Ver. farther abridge the view. Plant boldly, therefore, on
ſuch a brow, it is itſelf your object; its beauty muſt
ariſe from the richneſs of its veſture, and conſequently
the trees with which it is clothed muſt be cloſely
200 planted together; but on the plain beneath they muſt
be ſet ſingle, or at wide intervals, and this without
any ſeeming order or the viſible interference of art.

210 Art muſt, however, in reality interefere, and that for many purpoſes; the indiſcriminating hand might elſe exclude an eligible diſtance by the interpoſition of trees which ſpread their tops and hang their impenetrable branches, while, under her correction, the ſcene may be preſerved, and ſufficient wood obtained by planting only ſuch as bear an airy foliage on light and lofty ſtems.

219 She muſt ſuperintend the choice of trees deſtined to form either clumps or an extenſive ſhade, and for this purpoſe ſelect ſuch only as are of ſimilar character, ſize, and colour, and alſo bear their leaves in the ſame ſeaſon.

226 She will hearken to the dictates of Nature, and carefully avoiding every tranſgreſſion againſt her laws, will

will adapt her plants only to such soils and situations Ver.
as are favourable to their culture.

Avoiding disproportion, she will forbear to plant 232
the Lawn with low clumps of shrubbery, and, instead of incongruously attempting there to interpose their diminutive stature for the sake of variety, will range them contiguous to the pathway, where alone they can have consequence, and where the eye may either dwell upon their peculiar beauties, or altogether look beyond them.

She will teach us also to cultivate only the hardy 240
indigenous race of trees, and to avoid the introduction of exotics into the general scene, from which an ill-adapted climate will soon snatch them, and so
leave a blank. This doctrine the Poet has enforced 252
and exemplified in a fictitious tale, which, however, he concludes with a little abatement of his interdiction; for he allows, that if a taste for foreign plants must be gratified, it may be indulged in some lateral seclusion from the general scene sheltered from every rougher blast, and open only in mild and favorable aspects.

Ver.

301 The ſubject of planting being now concluded with
a very brief recapitulation, referring the particular
inſtances to good taſte, and limiting every precept
313 that would attempt to regulate this to little more than
prohibitory caution, a ſubſequent evil is ſuggeſted, which is the overgrowth of trees beyond the line they were intended to deſcribe, by means of which, when the effect is obtained it is almoſt as ſoon loſt; but the Planter whoſe materials (in this differing from thoſe of the Painter) will not retain their forms, is aſſured of his remedy in attention; and of being able to reſtore his outline by introducing the axe and pruning knife to cut off the luxuriance that has infringed thoſe limits which his pictureſque idea had originally preſcribed.

343 Care then, we perceive, is neceſſary to preſerve what
Taſte had created, but this neceſſity, we are told,
ſhould not yet diſcourage us from the purſuit of
beauty: Mutability is a common lot, and the poſſi-
349 bility of Winter-torrents might be equally well urged
350 againſt the introduction of Water into a Scene, or
that it is liable to be dried away by violent Summer
heats. And here the Poet, by means of this exempli-
354 fication, with great addreſs changes his theme from
Wood to WATER; he ſeems to pant beneath the fer-

vours

vours he has just described, and seeking a refuge in Ver.
the coolness of the element he has named, assumes
the latter as a subject which the heat he sustains has
rendered grateful to his mind.

The tendency which Nature has bestowed upon 359.
every portion of her works is vindicated to them as a
species of right, and that of Fluidity being an active
descent to the lowest beds, the false principles upon
which the French, as described by Rapin, have endeavoured to give an upward current to water by means
of Jet d'eaux, with all their fantastic varieties, are
censured as an infringement of its equitable claims;
while the dank bottom ground, which is, on that 379
account, unfavourable to vegetation, is declared to be
the proper receptacle of this element. Here then, if
sufficiently copious, let it spread; or, if more scantily 381
supplied, and that the declivity of the soil be such as 383
to afford it a channel, let it rather assume the form of
a river; for to this, Extent which is in general beyond
the reach of Art, and yet the usual character of natural
lakes, is not required. But, be the disposition what
it may, we are desired in either case to give to water 385
an air of freedom in its outline, and a bolder curve
than that which has been already prescribed for the
pathway; the natural reason of which precept is,

that

that the baſe of every little inequality in the ground jets into and turns it, and conſequently, as it is unable to climb and ſurmount theſe, it muſt receive them as limits to its bed or channel. Theſe, it is true, the torrent may cut or wear away, and hence the rocky and perpendicular bank has its original; but unleſs we have the means to ſupply a torrent ſpeed to our artificial rivers, this ſpecies of margin is not a proper ſubject for our imitation.

398 Though the river has obtainted a preference on account of the difficulty of giving ſufficient greatneſs to the lake, the latter is not, however, proſcribed, and the ſmalleſt extent of water is allowed of for the purpoſe of reflecting foliage and its accidents, and as a ſcene for Water-fowl, &c. provided that it be in a ſequeſtered ſituation, and well ſurrounded with foreſt-trees; but unleſs ſo bounded, theſe diminutive pools are declared to be abſolutely inadmiſſible, nothing being more obnoxious to the eye than ſuch palpable patches; for even the greateſt rivers, if by their windings they are rendered ſeemingly diſcontinuous, and are caught only at broken intervals, are adjudged diſguſting, being thus reduced to pools, unleſs indeed they afford a conſiderable ſtretch of water contiguous to the beholder's ſtation, in which caſe the eye is carried on

to their distances, and thus unites their divided parts Ver.
without any other assistance.

Fill then the channel you give to the water, pro- 415
vided the best effect of river is sought for, in order
that it may not be interrupted in its windings, but
still demonstrate its own continuance; but when this
has in reality found its determination, let the eye
there encounter some strong feature of wood or hill
seemingly interposed; for beyond this, if conducted
with judgment, the imagination will certainly con- 419
tinue to prolong the stream. And here a consideration
of the necessity we lie under of procuring abundant
supplies of water for all these purposes, leads the Poet
to a direct prohibition of every attempt to introduce
this great natural ornament, unless we can give it perfection from such supplies.

The flat lake and low-bedded river being thus dis- 423
missed, we now come to the rules which teach the
streams to descend with beauty from their higher
sources to the vallies underneath. But first, the false
taste of our ancestors, which conducted water thus
circumstanced down by steps, as it were, and for
resting-places, disposed it in short canals, so ranged
one beneath another as in profile to afford the appearance

ance of ſtairs, but of length and continuance from
ſome one favoured point of view, is cenſured as de-
429 ſerving only our contempt, which we ought to beſtow ſtill more liberally on that mode of communication which conveys it from thoſe above to thoſe
below by flights of narrow ſtairs, whether it is ſuffered
at all times to trickle down, or hoarded, on account
438 of its ſcarcity, to be devolved only at long and arbi-
trary intervals; for the caſcade, ſuch as Nature has
exhibited, and ſuch alone is recommended to our
preſent purpoſe, requires an abundant ſtore of water,
which muſt firſt be provided ere imitation is attempt-
450 ed, and inſtead of narrow ſteps requires a vaſt mound
462 to fall over (I), which, when raiſed, muſt have its
front beautified with rocks to ſhape the fall, and give
it the majeſtic rudeneſs of Nature. (K)

473 But as the poſſeſſion of theſe more magnificent
features of landſcape is beyond the limits of moſt
men's power, every attempt to atchieve them without
a previous certainty of ſucceſs is diſcouraged, and we
are deſired to acquieſce in the enjoyment of the little
rivulet which waters almoſt every ſcene; nay its improvement, if requiſite, is permitted; but this muſt
be made to correſpond exactly with its character: it
is not the office of genuine art here to ſtagnate the

lively

lively stream into width of lake, or by retarding its *Ver.*
current to give it the form of a slow-moving river; on 490
the contrary, she will try to fret, and so to increase
its murmuring course as to continue it still, only in a
higher degree, what Nature originally formed it.

On the secluded margin of one of these clear rivulets, the Poet presenting himself as seated, there testi-
fying the fitness of such a situation to excite Fancy,
and in a short history of his own life giving an instance how constantly he has been enamoured of this
kind of aquatic scenery, proceeds to confer a form
and voice upon the lovely stream that has so strongly
captivated his imagination. That voice which he
has thus bestowed, he accordingly makes her now
raise, and concludes the book with a recital of the
Song, in which she aptly renders the several qualities 531
of her little current so many examples of virtue to
human Nature: her reflection of the ray she receives 542
from the sun reads to man a lesson of gratitude; the
nurture afforded to every little flower that embroiders 546
her banks, of extensive benevolence; she seeks the
lowliest vale for the path of her waters, and thence
rebukes the aspiring career of Ambition; she calls 549
on Sloth to mark her brisk and unceasing current; 552
and swelling to an indignant torrent effectually to

Ver. resist the Tyranny of Art, contemptuously derides
555 the servile Spirit; she then commissions her Poet to
559 report her counsels, and with a warning voice to pronounce the vices she has reprobated to be the cause of a nation's overthrow; but, if neglected, himself to take the lesson and monopolize the profits he is denied the means of communicating; and thus we become almost persuaded that we find the assertion of Shakespear's Duke in *As you like it*, even literally verified, the little brook has instructed us in good;

" And thus a life exempt from public haunt
" Finds tongues in trees, books in the running streams,
" Sermons in stones, and good in every thing."

COM-

COMMENTARY

ON THE

FOURTH BOOK.

SIMPLICITY having already reformed the taste and corrected the false principles of Gardening; delineated the genuine curve of Nature; instructed us in the means of uniting Beauty with Use, and to this end concealed the necessary fence which forms their common limit; having promulged the laws of Planting, and directed the proper course or bed for Water, is once more invoked to continue her assistance, while the Poet proceeds now to the consideration of artificial ornaments, that is, of such works of Architecture and Sculpture as may, without derogation from its dignity, be admitted into the Garden Scene.

But this is not the whole, for the fourth Book not only extends to artificial ornament, but is a kind of recapitulation of all that has gone before, which, exclusive of variety, the declared purpose of its Author, gives, even in point of strict propriety, a preference to the form of a tale in which it is conceived; for were it preceptively written, it must have been restricted to its single subject, while the ordinary rules

Ver. of composition allow a latitude and allot the business of exemplification and enforcement to the conclusion. The demesne of ALCANDER accordingly shews us not the example only from which we may, on the present portion of the subject, deduce for ourselves the rule, but in its general disposition demonstrates the great advantage of attending to every rule that has been already prescribed.

These, however, have been considered in their respective places, and therefore it only remains for me to discuss the principles of artificial ornament as they are set forth in the practice of ALCANDER.

65 All vestiges of former Art being obliterated, and
Nature restored to her original simplicity, the study
of congruity in ornament is the first maxim that offers
itself to our observation; and, therefore, if the principal structure or mansion be Gothic, the ornamental
80 buildings should be made to agree with it. Even such necessary structures as the offices of a Farm, seldom ornamental in themselves, may, at a proper distance, receive this character; by being masked with the fictitious ruins of a castle they will appear as if the reliques of an antient fortress had been turned to the purposes of husbandry, and thus, instead of offending the

the sight, be converted to a correspondent and even a Ver.
noble object; while a mouldering Abbey will better 80
serve to conceal those domestic structures that stand 95
nearer to the view.

But not only the mutual agreement of buildings should be attended to, but their agreement with the circumstances of the scene in which they are introduced; the Castle, for instance, should derive the probability of having stood in former ages, from a situation in which it is probable that a former age would have placed it for the purposes of defence and strength; to this, therefore, an elevated situation is adapted, while a secluded recess and contiguity to running water, are not among the least essential characters of the Abbey, which should, now that time is supposed to have passed over it, stand backed with wood, and so sunk in shade as to give it an air of antique solemnity; for the great and venerable tree will be considered as a kind of witness to its age, while diligence should be used to bring forward the growth of Ivy to assist in giving credit to the fiction.

Still farther, in every ornamental building of whatsoever kind, an agreement of its parts among themselves is to be maintained; in those already instanced

it

VII. it is requisite that every character of each should be preserved with the most scrupulous precision: omission of parts indeed may be justified by the supposition of ruin and decay; but what can palliate the absurdity of annexing parts unknown to antiquity, and altogether foreign from the original purposes of such a structure.

These are the greatest possible artificial features, and as they must necessarily preclude all littleness, and consequently exceed the abilities of most improvers, they are converted to uses which must, undoubtedly, be somewhere complied with, and which will, therefore, defray at least some part of the charges. These also belong to the general scenery, and consequently admit of no dispensation either with respect to their greatness, or propriety in the manner of constructing them. The inference is obvious: where the execution, from its proper point of view, cannot amount to absolute deception, let the attempt be altogether relinquished: to fictitious buildings of this nature I have never yet heard an objection (and many an objection I have heard) that in substance extended farther than to such as are ill performed, and against such I am as ready to give my voice as the severest critic that has ever passed judgment upon them. (L)

But

But, apart from the general, there is alſo another Ver.
ſpecies of ſcenery to which alone the ornament may 119
be referred without conſidering its relation to the
whole: Thus, if the valley be ſo ſunk as to make no
part of the proſpect, the ſtructure that adorns it may
be adapted rather to this of which it will conſtitute
an important feature, than to the whole, of which,
by the ſuppoſition, it makes no part at all; to this
retired valley, therefore, if watered by a rapid ſtream,
the grotto is well adapted, for the water trickling thro'
its roof, will ſerve to keep it always cool for refreſh-
ment; but even here within itſelf, conſiſtency of ornament muſt be attended to; and whether the ſcene in
which it is placed be inland, or in view of the ocean,
the building muſt only be incruſted with the productions that are natural to its ſituation and the ſoil.

The Flower-Garden alſo comes under this deſcrip- 175
tion; and therefore it is required, that it ſhall ſtand
apart from the general ſcene, and be whatever it is
within itſelf; ſome glade or ſheltered ſecluſion is conſequently its proper ſituation. The form and diſpo- 194
ſition of the flower-beds, though very irregular, muſt
not appear broken into too many round and disjointed
patches, but only ſeem to interrupt the green-ſward
walks, which, like the mazy herbage that in foreſt-
ſcenes

Ver. ſcenes uſually ſurrounds the underwood tufts of
194 thorn, wind careleſsly among them, and running
from ſide to ſide through every part of the ſcene,
frequently meet the gravel path that leads round
the whole. The Flower-Garden being profeſſedly a
work of art, will no more deſire to catch proſpects
beyond its own limits than it ſeeks to be ſeen from
206 without itſelf; the internal ſcenery, therefore, muſt
conſiſt of objects adapted to a neighbouring eye, preſent it with graceful architectural forms, and call to
mind, by their emblems, the Virtues and the Arts that
deſerve our cultivation, or by their buſts the names of
men, who, by cultivating theſe, have deſerved our
grateful remembrance.

212 But among all the ornaments of the Flower-Garden,
the Conſervatory is intitled to the pre-eminence;
great, however, as it may be rendered, it is not yet
requiſite that its ſtyle ſhould coincide with that of the
manſion; it ſtands in a ſeparate ſcene, there forms
the principal feature, and, conſequently, inſtead of
receiving, ſhould itſelf preſcribe the mode to which
every inferiour ornament muſt be made to conform.

Separation from the general scene is likewise re- Ver.
quisite for the recess where domestic fowl are reared; 314
and as these are of two kinds, the land and the
aquatic, their little demesne must consist of parts
adapted to the habits of each: the lake studded with
small islands, and surrounded with a grassy bank, will
afford them every accommodation of this nature; and
the narrowness of the space required will give propriety 325
to the introduction of some classic emblematical ornaments; while the whole animated plot may be enjoyed 334
from a bower or rustic seat, so situated as at once to
comprehend it all, and so circumstanced as to shut out
the glare of the noontide sun by the means of climbing shrubbery, which will serve at the same time to
invest the wall and conceal the masonry of which this
bower must necessarily be constructed.

These three consistencies, for such they may be
called, with the scene, with each other, and of each
within itself, being thus declared necessary to artificial
ornaments, and exemplified in a Gothic scheme, the
manner of maintaining them, where the mansion or
principal structure is of Greek Architecture, is now 388
prescribed; and here, instead of the majestic Ruin,
the great ornaments of the general scene should rather
consist of the Temple, the Obelisk, the Column, or

Ver. triumphal Arch. The fragment, however, of the
388 Gothic Structure is not to be considered as an inconsistency in England; it may be the residue of an age that actually once existed; it has, consequently, a kind of prescriptive right to its station, and should not therefore be obliged to conform; while the Greek
400 buildings that are raised to suit the mansion must be made to appear its modern cotemporaries, the idea of a Greek Ruin in England being a contradiction both to history and experience.

403 Every argument to prove the necessity of maintaining consistency, being in a manner exhausted, it remained only for the Poet with ridicule to explode the heterogeneous miscellanies of buildings which have been sometimes drawn together from remote parts of the earth, and by a comic painting of the puerile chaos to render it contemptible in our eyes.

639 As it seems to have been our Author's intention to select from the variety of buildings, which have usually found a place in our modern Gardens, such as were capable of being introduced with the greatest congruity, and, when so introduced, capable of producing the best effect, he could not well overlook, that most common of them all, the Hermitage; he has therefore

therefore allotted to it a situation retired and solitary; *Ver.* but, as the melancholy circumstances of his tale led him to do, he has also made it a kind of monumental structure; here as elsewhere, both by example and precept, conveying to us these important lessons, that such melancholy memorials should only be raised where a real interest in their object gives them propriety, and that where the circumstance recorded is
near the heart, simplicity should be most studiously 648
consulted, as emblems and unappropriated ornaments must necessarily prove contemptible to a mind which is too much in earnest to derive any pleasure from fiction. (M)

Although it has been my province to divide what the Poet has most closely interwoven, to decompound, as it were, this part of the Poem, and separate the preceptive maxims from the tender narrative in which they are involved, I cannot, however, conclude without observing that this book appears to me to be *unique* in its kind, as combining with infinite address in one natural whole, the dramatic, the descriptive, and the didactic *genera* of writing. To elucidate the last is all that I have attempted; and if what I have written tends, in any sort, to give the less attentive kind of readers a clearer conception of the general plan

Ver. of the Poem, and of the connexion of its parts with each other, it will add considerably to the pleasure I have already enjoyed in this agreeable occupation.

665 Having now finished the whole of his subject, he concludes this book, as he had done the first, with an address to those of his countrymen who have a relish for the politer arts; but as an interval of more than ten years had past between the times when the first and fourth books were written, that art, therefore, which in the former he exhorts them to practice for the embellishment of a then prosperous country, in the
672 latter he recommends, merely for the purpose of amusement and self-consolation, at a period when the freedom and prosperity of that country lay oppressed beneath the weight of an immoral, a peculating, a sanguinary, and desolating system. History, when she transmits the records of the year 1781, will best convince posterity that this conclusion of the Poem had in it as much propriety when it was written, as they will feel that it has pathos when they peruse it.

It is reserved for me to conclude this Commentary in a happier hour: When a great and unexpected ministerial revolution gives us good reason to hope that the sword which was drawn to obliterate the rights of mankind, and cut up the ſecurities of Property, will ſoon hide its diſappointed and guilty edge in its ſcabbard; that commerce will once more return with opulence to our ſhores; and that a juſt, a generous, and a liberal Policy will ſcorn to reſtrain her benefits to a ſingle diſtrict of a great and united Empire. I have only to aſk of Heaven to haſten the maturity of theſe bleſſings; to give them perpetuity; and, inſtead of ſuffering a barbarous and debilitating luxury to grow upon that proſperity of which it has thus afforded us a proſpect, to invigorate our very amuſements, and teach us with a manly and patriot pride, in the hours of peace and relaxation, to aim at liſting our country to that ſuperiority in genuine Arts which we have ſo lately begun to vindicate to her in juſt and honourable Arms.

THE END OF THE COMMENTARY.

MAY 30, 1782.

NOTES

UPON THE

POEM

AND

COMMENTARY.

Such of the following Notes as are marked with numeral Letters and the number of the Verse refer to the Poem; and were inserted by the Author in the former quarto Editions of its separate books. Those marked with the capital Letters of the Alphabet and the Page refer to the Commentary.

NOTES.

UPON

BOOK THE FIRST

And its COMMENTARY.

NOTE I. Verſe 30.

At this ſad hour, my deſolated ſoul.

THIS Poem was begun in the year 1767, not long after the death of the amiable perſon here mentioned. *See Epitaph the firſt in the Author's Poems.*

NOTE A. Page 121.

I think it proper to apprize my Reader, that I uſe the general term GARDENING for that peculiar ſpecies of modern improvement which is the ſubject of the Poem, as it is diſtinguiſhed from common horticulture and planting.——The Gardener in my ſenſe, and in that of the Poet, bears the ſame relation to the Kitchen-Gardener that the Painter does to the Houſe-Painter.

NOTE B. Page 130.

The few deſcriptions of Gardens which occur in the writers of antiquity, cut off all hope of obtaining any claſſical aid to the art. In that of Alcinous the

B b charm

charm consists not in the happy disposition of the little plot, for it was hedged in and contained only four acres, but in the supernatural eternity of its bloom and verdure, and the perpetual maturity of its fruits. The hanging gardens of Babylon, and of the Egyptian Thebes, like the pastures on the roof of Nero's golden palace, are rather to be considered as the caprices of Architecture. The younger Cyrus, according to Xenophon's account of his occupations, had, perhaps, a more just idea of magnificence, yet still the orderly arrangement of his quincunxes could never have consisted with the picturesque principle. If we turn to the primitive Romans, their Agrarian laws, however ill executed, directly operated against this art, and we find Cincinatus called not from his Garden but his Farm to assume the government of his county; and as to the Liternum of Scipio, that simplicity of life, which is so highly applauded by Seneca, and the very little care he took even to accommodate himself there, will give us reason to believe that he rather neglected than overpolished his villa. Cicero was a professed admirer of *topiary works*, which exactly correspond with the green statuary, the espaliers, and trellis-work of our own old gardens: "Trahitur enim Cupressus in "picturas opere historiali, venatus classesve, et ima-

"gines

" gines rerum tenui folio, brevique et virente fuper-
" veftiens." *Plin. Nat. Hift. lib.* 6. *cap.* 33.

From the laboured defcription which the Younger Pliny has given us of his own Thufcan Villa, we may at once infer the truth of our Poet's panegyric on the general appearance of Italy, and alfo that Gardening had not improved at Rome beneath the imperial yoke. Nothing can exceed the beauty of that fcenery which this elegant writer has laid before us: " A " Theatre, fuch as Nature alone could conftruct, is " prefented to our eye: a Valley is extended at the " foot of the furrounding Appenine, whofe loftieft " fummits are crowned with old patrician Forefts, " while the defcending fides are covered with foliage, " there only interrupted where fome bold projections " lift their heads above it: Vineyards extended on " every fide occupy the bafe of the mountain, while " the valley beneath looks chearful with meadows and " cornfields, and all the varieties of inclofure and cul- " tivation; the whole is fertilized by eternal rills " which are yet no where collected in a ftagnant lake, " but hurry down the declivities of the ground into " the Tiber, which, forming here a vaft navigable " ftream, and reflecting the whole landfcape from his " fmooth furface, divides the valley in the midft."

Such are the glowing ſcenes of Italy, and how well adapted they are to the canvas Pliny himſelf has perceived; for he declares, "the view before him to "reſemble a picture beautifully compoſed rather than "a work of Nature accidentally delivered."

And now having contemplated the proſpect, it is time to turn our eye to the proprietor, and the character of that foreground from which he was pleaſed to enjoy it. Behold him then hemmed in by a narrow incloſure, ſurrounded with a graduated mound, tracing, perhaps, his own or his Gardener's name ſcribbled in ſome ſort of herbage upon a formal parterre, or ranging in allies formed of boxen pyramids and unſhorn apple-trees placed alternately, in order, as he declares himſelf, "happily to blend ruſticity "with the works of more poliſhed art;" nay, it is even poſſible that ſeated now upon a perforated bench, ſo contrived as, under the preſſure of his weight, to fling up innumerable jets d'eau, he thence takes in the view of this "vaſt Theatre of "Nature" from between the figures of fantaſtic monſters or the jaws of wild beaſts, into which he has ſhorn a row of box-trees at the foot of an even ſloping terras. In brief, in a foreground probably deſigned, but certainly applauded by the Younger Pliny,

Pliny, no veſtige of Nature is ſuffered to remain; and if, from a man of his erudition and accompliſhments, we receive no better a model for our imitation, I believe we may ſafely infer, that however lovely Italian ſcenery in general may be to the eye, the ſearch of claſſic aid to the Art of Gardening muſt prove abſolutely fruitleſs: By one of his contemporaries, it is true, the defective taſte of his age was obſerved, but the cenſure affords an argument of its univerſality while it exempts only the ſenſible individual who pronounced it.

In vallem Egeriæ deſcendimus et ſpeluncas
Diſſimileis veris. Quanto præſtantius eſſet
Numen Aquæ, viridi ſi margine clauderet undas
Herba, nec ingenuum violarent marmora tophum.

Juven. Sat. iii. *ver.* 17.

The villa of the Gordiani, deſcribed by J. Capitolinus, is in much the ſame ſtile, nor does that of Diocleſian ſeem to have poſſeſſed any advantage over it.

I ſhould not name the fictitious Garden of Pſyche, as delineated in very general terms by Apuleius, but for the purpoſe of introducing one of a much later date, deſcribed by his commentator Beroaldus, and

ſo

ſo illuſtrating the equally defective Taſte of modern "ſuperſtitious Italy." "Behold then the faireſt and moſt magnificent ſeat ſubſiſting in the territories of Bologna in the year 1510; and we find its beauties to conſiſt of a marble fountain, in a green incloſure, throwing the water up by the means of ſiphons; of a fiſh-pond annexed to this; and of a long and right-lined canal between two parallel ſtone-walls, while another ſtone-wall of ten feet high, but broad enough at top to admit of two perſons walking abreaſt on it, completely excludes the view of the country and of the natural river from which this canal is ſupplied with water." In the year 1550 we find a Cardinal á Valle, at Rome, employed in erecting a hanging Garden on the columns of his palace. Strada, who was himſelf a Roman, gives us his own idea of a perfect Garden in the middle of the laſt century, and like that of Pliny, it principally conſiſts of jets d'eau and green ſtatuary: And Biſhop Burnet, in the year 1685, deſcribes the Borromean Garden in the Lago Maggiore, as "riſing from the lake by five rows of "terraſſes on the three ſides of the Garden that are "watered by the lake; the ſtairs are noble, the walls "are all covered with Oranges and Citrons, and a "more beautiful ſpot of a Garden cannot be ſeen." He afterwards informs us, in more general terms, that

"the

" the Gardens of Italy are made at great coſt: the " ſtatues and fountains are very rich and noble; the " grounds are well laid out, and the walks are long and " even, but they are ſo high-ſcented by plots made " with box, that there is no pleaſure to walk in them; " they alſo lay their walks between hedges that one " is much confined in them. In many of their Gar- " dens there goes a courſe of water round the walls, " about a foot from the ground, in a channel of ſtone " that goes round the ſide of the wall." So here is an Italian Garden, walled round, watered by fountains, and an elevated ſtone-channel at its extremities, and divided into box-plots by long, even, high-hedged walks; " but they have no gravel," he ſays, " to " make theſe firm and beautiful like thoſe we have " in England;" and hence, perhaps, it is that the judgment of Addiſon, who viſited that country but a little after, may be accounted for; " for he ſays, " their Gardens then contained a large extent of " ground covered over with an agreeable mixture of " Garden and Foreſt, which repreſent every where an " artificial rudeneſs, much more charming than that " neatneſs and elegance which we meet with in our " own country;" but he beſtows the ſame encomium upon the Gardens of France, where there is but little reaſon to believe that he really found a better ſtile

than

than that which prevailed at home; he desired to reform a mode that disgusted him; he saw the fault and wished to avoid it, but had never formed an idea of the perfection to which it was possible the art could be carried; whatever differed from the obnoxious track he had been used to afforded him satisfaction, and this he probably exaggerated to himself, and was glad to make use of as an example to his doctrines. It is not very likely that Mr. Addison, if he were still living, would now bestow the exalted title of heroic Poets upon the designers of Kensington Gardens: But the fact is, we were in his time the apes of France in this as well as in every other frippery device of Fashion, and Le Nautre alike presided over the taste of Gardening in both countries Rapin is childish in his precepts; Stevens, a century before him, delivered nearly the same in prose; and I cannot find that France, at any previous time, afforded an instance of a practice better than they have prescribed. The genius of Petrarch, I grant, is in some respect visible at Vaucluse; but who has dared to tread in his footsteps? But I do not design minutely to trace the history of French Gardening. It is my purpose only to confirm the assertion of the Poet, who vindicates the Art he sings to his own country; and this, I think, I have sufficiently done, by enquiring into its

state

ſtate upon the Continent, and chiefly in Italy, down to the time about which it ſeems to have had its commencement in England; but though admired by ſome of their travellers who have viſited this country, it is not yet adopted by them, and conſequently no modern claim can come into competition with ours. Mr. Gray has aſſerted our originality in this particular, and Algarotti has acknowledged it *. The Art is, therefore, our own, and conſequently the Poem, which undertakes to impart its principles, has a right to intitle itſelf the ENGLISH GARDEN.

NOTE C. Page 141.

In a poſtſcript which the Author annexed to the quarto edition of the fourth book of this Poem, in which he gave a general analyſis of the whole, and anſwered certain objections which had been made to particular paſſages in it, he thus vindicates himſelf for having preſcribed the demolition of viſtas, which had been defended as having in themſelves a conſiderable ſhare of intrinſic beauty: "I am," ſays he, "myſelf far from denying this, I only aſſert that their beauty is not pictureſque beauty; and, therefore, that it is to be rejected by thoſe who follow pictureſque principles. It is architectural beauty, and accords

 only

* See Memoirs of the Life and Writings of Mr. Gray, Let. 8. Sect. 5.

only with architectural works. Where the Artist follows those principles, vistas are certainly admissible; and the French, who have so long followed them, have, therefore, not improperly (though one cannot help smiling at the title) given us, in their Dictionary of Sciences, an article of *Architecture du Jardinage.* But did Gaspar Poussin, or Claude Lorrain, ever copy those beauties on their canvas? Or would they have produced a picturesque effect by their means if they had? I think this single consideration will induce every person of common taste to allow that these two principles oppose one another; and that whenever they appear together, they offend the eye of the beholder by their heterogenous beauty. If, therefore, vistas are ever to be admitted, or rather to be retained, it is only where they form an approach to some superb mansion so situated that the principal prospect and ground allotted to picturesque improvement lie entirely on the other side; so much so that the two different modes of planting can never appear together from any given point of view; and this is the utmost that I can concede on the subject."

NOTE II. Verse 395.

With stone. Egregious madness; yet pursu'd

Altho' this seems to be the principle upon which

this

this falſe taſte was founded, yet the error was detected by one of our firſt writers upon architecture. I ſhall tranſcribe the paſſage, which is the more remarkable as it came from the quaint pen of Sir Henry Wotton: "I muſt note," ſays he, "a certain contrariety be-"tween building and gardening: for as fabricks "ſhould be regular, ſo gardens ſhould be irregular, "or at leaſt caſt into a very wild regularity. To ex-"emplify my conceit, I have ſeen a garden, for the "manner perchance incomparable, into which the "firſt acceſs was a high walk like a terras, from "whence might be taken a general view of the whole "plot below, but rather in a delightful confuſion, "than with any plain diſtinction of the pieces. "From this the beholder deſcending many ſteps, was "afterwards conveyed again by ſeveral mountings "and valings, to various entertainments of his ſcent "and ſight: which I ſhall not need to deſcribe, for "that were poetical; let me only note this, that "every one of theſe diverſities, was as if he had been "magically tranſported into a new garden." Were the terras and the ſteps omitted, this deſcription would ſeem to be almoſt entirely conformable to our preſent ideas of ornamental planting. The paſſage, which follows is not leſs worthy of our notice. "But tho' "other countries have more benefit of the Sun than

" we, and thereby more properly tied to contemplate " this delight; yet have I ſeen in our own a delicate " and diligent curioſity, ſurely without parallel among " foreign nations, namely in the garden of Sir Henry " Fanſhaw, at his ſeat in Ware-Park; where, I well " remember, he did ſo preciſely examine the tinctures " and ſeaſons of his flowers, that in their ſettings, " the inwardeſt of which that were to come up at the " ſame time, ſhould be always a little darker than " the utmoſt, and ſo ſerve them for a kind of gentle " ſhadow." This ſeems to be the very ſame ſpecies of improvement which Mr. Kent valued himſelf for inventing, in later times, and of execuing, not indeed with flowers, but with flowering ſhrubs and evergreens, in his more finiſhed pieces of ſcenery. The method of producing which effect has been deſcribed with great preciſion and judgment by a late ingenious writer. (See *Obſervations on modern Gardening*, ſect. 14th, 15th, and 16th.) It may, however, be doubted whether Sir Henry Fanſhaw's garden were not too *delicate* and *diligent* a curioſity, ſince its panegyriſt concludes the whole with telling us, that it was " like a piece not of Nature, but of Art." See *Reliquiæ Wottonianæ*, page 64, edit. 4th.

NOTE

Note III. Verſe 412.

The wilds of taſte. Yes, ſageſt Verulam,

Lord Bacon, in the 46th of his eſſays, deſcribes what he calls *the platform of a princely garden.* If the Reader compare this deſcription with that which Sir William Temple has given in his eſſay, intituled, *The Gardens of Epicurus,* written in a ſubſequent age, he will find the ſuperiority of the former very apparent; for though both of them are much obſcured by the falſe taſte of the times in which they were written, yet the vigor of Lord Bacon's genius breaks frequently through the cloud, and gives us a very clear diſplay of what the real merit of gardening would be when its true principles were aſcertained. For inſtance, out of thirty acres which he allots for the whole of his Pleaſure-ground, he ſelects the firſt four for a lawn, without any intervention of plot or parterre, "becauſe," ſays he, "nothing is more plea-"ſant to the eye than green graſs kept finely ſhorn." And "as for the making of knots of figures, with "diverſe coloured earths, that they may lie under "the windows of the houſe, on that ſide which the "garden ſtands, they be but toys, you may ſee as "good ſights many times in tarts." Sir William Temple, on the contrary, tells us, that in the garden at Moor-park, which was his model of perfection, the firſt inlet to the whole was a very broad gravel walk garniſhed with a row of Laurels which looked like Orange-trees, and was terminated at each end by a ſummer-houſe. The parterre or principal garden which makes the ſecond part in each of their deſcriptions, it muſt be owned, is equally devoid of ſimplicity in them both. "The garden," ſays his Lordſhip, "is beſt to be ſquare, encompaſſed with a ſtately "arched-hedge, the arches to be upon carpenters "work, over every arch a little belly enough to re-"ceive a cage of birds, and, over every ſpace, be-"tween the arches, ſome other little figure with "broad plates of round coloured glaſs, gilt for the "ſun to play upon." It would have been difficult for Sir William to make his more fantaſtic; he has, however, not made it more natural. The third part, which Lord Bacon calls the Heath, and the other the Wilderneſs, is that in which the Genius of Lord Bacon is moſt viſible; "for this," ſays he, "I wiſh "to be framed as much as may be to a natural wild-"neſs." And accordingly he gives us a deſcription of it in the moſt agreeable and picturеſque terms, inſomuch that it ſeems leſs the work of his own fancy than a delineation of that ornamental ſcenery which had no exiſtence till above a century after it was written. Such, when he deſcended to matters

of

of mere Elegance (for when we ſpeak of Lord Bacon, to treat of theſe was to deſcend) were the amazing powers of his univerſal Genius.

NOTE IV. Verſe 447.

All that the Nymph forgot, or left forlorn.

See Spencer's Fairy Queen, Book 4th, Canto the 10th: the paſſage immediately alluded to is in the 21ſt Stanza.

For all that Nature, by her mother wit,
Could frame in earth and form of ſubſtance baſe
Was there; and all that Nature did omit,
Art (playing Nature's ſecond part) ſupplied it.

NOTE V. Verſe 453.

That work, " where not nice Art in curious knots,

See Milton's inimitable deſcription of the garden of Eden. Paradiſe Loſt, Book 4th, part of which is here inſerted.

NOTE VI. Verſe 481.

Thou reach the Orchard, where the ſparing turf

The French at preſent ſeem to be equally ſparing of this natural clothing of the earth, although they have done us the honour to adopt our Bowling-greens, and to improve upon them. This appears from the following

following article of the Encyclopedie tranflated verbatim.

" Boulingrin. N. S. In gardening is a fpecies of
" Parterre compofed of pieces of divided turf with
" borders floping (*en glacis*) and evergreens at the
" corners and other parts of it. It is mowed four
" times a year to make the turf finer. The invention
" of this kind of parterre comes from England, as
" alfo its name, which is derived from *Boule*, round,
" and *Grin*, fine grafs or turf. Boulingrins are either
" fimple or compound; the fimple are all turf with-
" out ornament; the compound are cut into com-
" partments of turf, embroidered with knots, mixt
" with little paths, borders of flowers, yew-trees,
" and flowering fhrubs. Sand alfo of different colours
" contributes greatly to their value."

NOTE VII. Verfe 489.

Surpaffing rule and order." TEMPLE, *yes*,

The paffage here alluded to is as follows: " What
" I have faid of the beft forms of Gardens is meant
" only of fuch as are in fome fort regular; *for there*
" *may be other forms wholly irregular, that may, for*
" *ought I know, have more beauty than any of the others*;
" but they muft owe it to fome extraordinary difpo-
" fitions of Nature in the feat, or fome great race of
" fancy

" fancy and judgment in the contrivance, which may " reduce many disagreeing parts into some figure " which shall yet upon the whole be very agreeable. " Something of this I have seen in some places, and " heard more of it from others who have lived much " among the Chineses." Sir William then gives us a kind of general account of the Chinese taste, and of their *Sharawadgi*, and concludes thus: " But I " should hardly advise any of these attempts in the " figure of gardens among us, they are adventures of " too hardy atchievement for any common hands; " and tho' there may be more honour if they succeed " well, yet there is more dishonour if they fail, and " it is twenty to one they will, whereas in regular " figures it is hard to make any great and remarkable " faults." *See Temple's Miscellanies*, vol. I. p. 186. fol. edit.

NOTE VIII. Verse 493.

Led to the fair atchievement. ADDISON,

I had before called Bacon the prophet, and Milton the herald of true taste in Gardening. The former, because in developing the constituent properties of a princely garden, he had largely expatiated upon that adorned natural wildness which we now deem the essence of the art. The latter, on account of his having made this natural wildness the leading idea in his exquisite description of Paradise. I here call Addison, Pope, Kent, &c. the Champions of this true taste, because they absolutely brought it into execution. The beginning therefore of an actual reformation may be fixed at the time when the Spectator first appeared. The reader will find an excellent chapter upon this subject in the Pleasures of Imagination, published in N°. 414 of the Spectator; and also another paper written by the same hand, N°. 447; but perhaps nothing went further towards destroying the absurd taste of clipped evergreens than the fine ridicule upon them in the 173d Guardian, written by Mr. Pope.

NOTE IX. Verse 503.

Sweeps thro' each kindred Vista; Groves to Groves

See Mr. Pope's Epistle on False Taste, inscribed to the Earl of Burlington. Few readers, I suppose, need be informed that this line alludes to the following couplet:

Grove nods to Grove, each alley has a brother,
And half the platform just reflects the other.

NOTE X. Verse 511.

The pencil's power: but, fir'd by higher forms

It is said that Mr. Kent frequently declared he caught his taste in Gardening from reading the pic-

turesque

turesque descriptions of Spenser. However this may be, the designs which he made for the works of that poet are an inconteſtible proof, that they had no effect upon his executive powers as a painter.

NOTE XI. Verse 522.

The simple Farm eclips'd the Garden's pride,

Mr. Southcote was the introducer, or rather the inventor of the *Ferme ornè*; for it may be presumed, that nothing more than the term is of French extraction.

NOTE D. Page 145.

Camden, who lived in the days of Spenser, has described Guy-Cliffe, in Warwickshire, in a manner that looks as if either the Taste of his time was infinitely superior to that of the period immediately succeeding it; or at least as if the Proprietor were himself an instance of a Genius very far transcending all his cotemporaries. "Guy-Cliffe, nunc Thomæ de Bello Fago habitatio, & quæ ipsa sedes est amænitatis: Nemusculum ibi est opacum, fontes limpidi et gemmei, antra muscosa, prata semper verna, rivi levis et susurrans per saxa discursus, nec non solitudo, et quies Musis amicissima." Here is nothing fantastic and unnatural, which is the more extraordinary, as Guy-Cliffe is situated in the same county with Ken-

 nelworth,

nelworth, at that time the principal ſeat of every quaint and ſumptuous departure from Nature and Simplicity.

Theobalds, which Hentzner has deſcribed, was laid out by Lord Burleigh, who ſeems to have anticipated all the abſurdities we uſually aſcribe to a Taſte ſuppoſed to have been long after imported from Holland; a Ditch full of water, Labyrinths made with a great deal of labour, and a Jet d'eau with its marble baſon, conſtitute the principal ornaments of the place; and in a ſtill earlier period, we learn that the Beauty of Nonſuch, the Delight of Henry VIII. conſiſted chiefly in Groves ornamented with trellis work, and cabinets of verdure. "At Ulſkelf, near Towton," ſays Leland, "there lives a Prebendary of York, poſſeſſed of a goodly orchard with walks *opere topiario*;" and, in the year 1538, the ſame author deſcribes "the Gardens within, and the orchards without the Mote" of Wreſchill-Caſtle, the antient ſeat of the Perceys, to have "been exceedingly fair. And in the orchards were mounts *opere topiario*, writhen about with degrees like turnings of cokil-ſhells to cum to the top without pain."

This is all that I will add to Mr. Maſon's notes on this part of the ſubject; I had intended to have gone a great deal farther, and to have traced the hiſtory of modern

modern Gardening in England as far as diligence would have fupplied me with materials; but the fubject has had the better fortune to come under the agreeable, the lively, and at the fame time the accurate pen of Mr. Walpole. With all my readers I rejoice that I have been thus prevented.

NOTES

NOTES

UPON

BOOK THE SECOND

And its COMMENTARY.

NOTE XII. Verse 10.

Which fills the fields with plenty. Hail that Art

THIS simile, founded on the vulgar error concerning the Harvest Moon, however false in philosophy, may, it is hoped, be admitted in poetry.

NOTE E. Page 152.

This rule is founded in Nature and Reason, and its universal application has the sanction of antiquity to support it. Quintilian, though certainly defective in his taste for Landscape, and even an admirer of *topiary* works, has yet in the following passage very well apologized for that regularity which he in general applauds, by making Utility and Profit, in these particular instances, reasons for it. "Nullusne *fructiferis* adhibendus est decor? quis neget? nam et in ordinem

dinem certaque intervalla redigam meas arbores: quid enim illo quincunxe speciosius, qui, in quamcunque partem spectaveris, rectus est? sed protinus in id quoque prodest ut terræ succum æqualiter trahant. Decentior Equus cujus adstricta sunt ilia, si idem velocior. Pulcher aspectu sit Athleta cujus lacertos exercitatio expressit, idem certamini paratior. Nunquam vero Species ab Utilitate dividitur." *Quint. Inst.* lib. viii. cap. iii. *de Ornatu.*

Cicero has elegantly observed, " Nullam partem corporis (vel hominis vel ceterarum animantium) sine aliqua necessitate affictam, totamque formam quasi perfectam reperietis Arte non casu. Quid in arboribus, in quibus non truncus, non rami, non folia sunt denique, nisi ad suam retinendam, conservandamque Naturam? nusquam tamen est ulla pars nisi venusta. Linquamus Naturam, Artesque videamus; quid tam in Navigio necessarium quam latera, quam carinæ, quam mali, quam vela? quæ tamen hanc habent in specie venustatem, ut non solum salutis sed etiam voluptatis causâ inventa esse videantur. Columnæ & templa & porticus sustinent, tamen habent non plus Utilitatis quam Dignitatis. Capitolii fastigium illud & cæterarum Ædium non Venustas sed Necessitas ipsa fabricata est. Nam cum esset habita ratio quemamodum ex utraque parte tecti

aqua

aqua delaberetur, Utilitatem Templi, Faſtigii Dignitas conſequuta eſt, ut etiam, ſi in Cœlo Capitolium ſtatueretur ubi imber eſſe non poſſet, nullam ſine Faſtigio dignitatem habiturum fuiſſe videatur. Hoc in omnibus item partibus Orationis evenit ut Utilitatem ac prope Neceſſitatem ſuavitas quædam & Lepos conſequatur." *Ciceron. de Oratore*, lib. iii.

I might multiply quotations without end, but will cloſe with a paſſage from the practical Architect Vitruvius, which may ſerve as a comment on the above beautiful obſervation of Cicero: "Quod non poteſt in veritate fieri, id non putaverent (Antiqui) in imaginibus factum, poſſe etiam rationem habere. Omnia enim certâ proprietate, & a veris Naturæ deductis moribus traduxerunt in operum perfectiones; & ea probaverunt, quorum Explicationes in diſputationibus rationem poſſunt habere Veritatis." *Vitruv.* lib. iv. cap. ii. *de Ornamentis Columnarum.*

Note XIII. Verſe 119.

Than does this ſylvan Deſpot. Yet to thoſe

See Book the Firſt, line 84. See alſo Mr. Pope's Epiſtle to Lord Burlington, line 57,

Conſult the Genius of the place in all, &c.

A fundamental rule, which is here further enlarged upon from line 126.

NOTE XIV. Verſe 222.

(And that the tyrant's plea) to work your harm.

Alluding to Milton.

So ſpake the Fiend, and with *neceſſity*,
The tyrant's plea, excus'd his dev'liſh deeds.
PARADISE LOST, book iv. line 393.

NOTE XV. Verſe 327.

Is curb'd by mimic ſnares; the ſlendereſt twine

Linnæus makes this a characteriſtical property of the fallow deer; his words are, *arcetur ſilo horizontali.* (See Syſt. Nat. Art. *Dama.*) I have ſometimes ſeen feathers tied to this line for greater ſecurity, though perhaps unneceſſarily. They ſeem, however, to have been in uſe in Virgil's time, from the following paſſage in the Georgicks:

Stant circumfuſa pruinis
Corpora magna boum: confertoque agmine cervi
Torpent mole novâ, et ſummis vix cornibus extant.
Hos non emiſſis canibus, non caſſibus ullis,
Puniceæve agitant pavidos formidine pennæ:
Sed fruſtra oppoſitum trudentes pectore montem
Cominus obtruncant ferro.
GEORG. lib. iii. v. 368.

Ruæus's comment on the fifth line is as follows: *linea, aut funiculus erat, cui Plumæ implicabantur variis tinctæ coloribus, ad feras terrendas, ut in retia agerentur.* And a ſimile, which Virgil uſes in the twelfth book of the Æneid, v. 749, and another in Lucan's Pharſ. lib. iv. v. 437, clearly prove that the learned Jeſuit has rightly explained the paſſage.

NOTE F. Page 159.

I omitted, in the Commentary, to take notice of the Feathers which the Author has mentioned as a means of reſtraining deer, becauſe in the foregoing Note he ſeemed to think them unneceſſary; and therefore I conceived that he introduced them only as a poetical embelliſhment founded merely on claſſical authority; but I have ſince learned that the practice ſtill prevails in many, perhaps all of our Engliſh foreſts, particularly in that of Whittlebury. It ſhould ſeem, therefore, that its continuance thro' ages muſt be ſupported by experience of its uſe, and that a horizontal line without theſe feathers would not be a ſufficient obſtruction.

NOTE

NOTE XVI. Verse 470.

The wise Sidonian liv'd: and, tho' the pest

ABDALONIMUS. The fact, on which this Episode is founded, is recorded by Diodorus Siculus, Plutarch, Justin, and Q. Curtius; the last is here chiefly followed. M. de Fontenelle and the Abbé Metastasio have both of them treated the subject dramatically.

NOTE G. Page 164.

Φοβερὸς γεωργὸς οὐδενί, φίλος πᾶσιν, ἄπειρος αἵματος, ἄπειρος σφαγῆς, ἱερὸς καὶ παναγὴς θεῶν ἐπικαρπίων καὶ ἐπιπληναίων καὶ ἀλώων καὶ προηροσίων· ἴσος μὲν ἐν δημοκρατίᾳ, ὀλιγαρχίαν δὲ καὶ τυραννίδα πάντων μάλιστα μίσει γεωργία.

Γεωργοὶ πρῶτοι μὲν τῶν εκ γῆς καρπῶν τοῖς δεδωκάσι θεοῖς ἀπερξάμενοι—γεωργῶν φιλάνθρωποι μὲν αἱ εὐχαι, εὔφημοι δὲ αἱ θυσίαι ἀπ᾽ οἰκείων πόνων, ἄμοιροι συμφορῶν, ἄμοιροι κακῶν.

Maxim. Tyr. Dissertat. xiv.

NOTES

UPON

BOOK THE THIRD

And its COMMENTARY.

NOTE H. Page 165.

THE respect Mr. Gray had for the Art of Gardening, appears in his letter to Mr. How, to which I have before referred my reader, (see Note B. p. 102.) but which I shall here insert at large, because I have since been informed that a Poem on the same subject has been lately published in France, and is there highly esteemed, in which the Author, like the rest of his countrymen, ascribes the origin of our Gardens to the Chinese. "He (Count Algarotti) is highly civil to our nation, but there is one point in which he does not do us justice; I am the more solicitous about it, because it relates to the only taste we can call our own; the only proof of our original talent in matter of pleasure, I mean our skill in Gardening, or rather laying out grounds: and this is no small honour to us, since neither France nor Italy have ever

had

had the leaſt notion of it, nor yet do at all comprehend it when they ſee it. That the Chineſe have this beautiful art in high perfection ſeems very probable from the Jeſuit's Letters, and more from Chambers's little diſcourſe publiſhed ſome years ago; but it is very certain we copied nothing from them, nor had any thing but Nature for our model. It is not forty years ſince the Art was born among us, and as ſure we then had no information on this head from China at all." *See Memoirs of Mr. Gray, Section* v. *Letter* viii.

In the laſt ſmaller Edition of Mr. Walpole's Anecdotes of Painting, the reader will alſo find a very entertaining and important addition made to his hiſtory of Gardening on this very ſubject (ſee vol. iv. p. 283.) which puts the matter out of all doubt. Yet it is to be obſerved, that Mr. Gray and Mr. Walpole differ in their ideas of Chineſe perfection in this Art: But had Mr. Gray lived to ſee what he calls Chambers's *little diſcourſe* enlarged into a *diſſertation on oriental Gardening* by Sir William Chambers, Knight, it is more than probable he would have come over to his friend's ſentiments; certain it is he would never have agreed with the French, in calling this ſpecies of Gardening *Le gout Anglo-Chinois.*

NOTE

Note XVII. Verſe 12.

Place I the Urn, the Buſt, the ſculptur'd Lyre,

Mr. Gray died July 31ſt, 1771. This book was begun a few months after. The three following lines allude to a ruſtic alcove the author was then building in his garden, in which he placed a medallion of his friend, and an urn; a lyre over the entrance with the motto from Pindar, which Mr. Gray had prefixt to his Odes, ΦΩΝΑΝΤΑ ΣΥΝΕΤΟΙΣΙ, and under it on a tablet this ſtanza, taken from the firſt edition of his Elegy written in a country church-yard.

Here ſcatter'd oft, the lovelieſt of the year,
By hands unſeen, are ſhowers of violets found;
The Redbreaſt loves to build and warble *here*,
And little footſteps lightly print the ground.

Note XVIII. Verſe 122.

Let England prize this daughter of the Eaſt

Our common Laurel was firſt brought into the Low Countries A. D. 1576 (together with the Horſe Cheſnut) from Conſtantinople, as a preſent from David Ungnad, the Imperial Ambaſſador in Turkey, to Cluſius the famous Botaniſt. It was ſent to him by the name of Trabiſon-Curmaſi, or the Date of Trebiſond, but he named it Lauro-Ceraſus.

NOTE XIX. Verſe 354.

Deepen your dripping roofs! this feveriſh hour

Theſe lines were written in June, 1778, when it was remarkably hot weather.

NOTE XX. Verſe 366.

Shuts to the tuneful trifling of the Bard,

René Rapin, a learned Jeſuit of the laſt century, who wrote a didactic Latin Poem on Gardens, in four books, by way of ſupplement to Virgil's Georgics. The third book treats the ſubject of water, or more properly of water-works, for it is entirely made up of deſcriptions of jets d'eau, and ſuch ſort of artificial baubles.

NOTE XXI. Verſe 388.

And winds with ſhorter bend. To drain the reſt

See Book the ſecond, ver. 50 to ver. 78, where the curve of beauty, or a line waving very gently, is ſaid not only to prevail in natural pathways, but in the courſe of rivulets and the outline of lakes. It generally does ſo; yet in the latter it is ſometimes found more abrupt: in artificial pieces of water, therefore, ſharper curves may be employed than in the formation of the ſand or gravel-walk.

Note XXII. Verſe 452.

That facile mode which His inventive powers

Mr. Brindley, who executed the Duke of Bridgewater's canal, and invented a method of making dams to hold water, without clay, uſing for this purpoſe any ſort of earth duly tempered with water.

Note I. Page 176.

The method of conſtructing theſe mounds, which is called "puddling," conſiſts only in greatly moiſtening and turning the ſoil (of whatever nature it may be) in the manner in which mortar is tempered; for thus its parts are brought cloſer together, and in its almoſt fluid ſtate the influence of attraction is allowed to operate, to turn to each other and bring into contact thoſe ſurfaces which are beſt adapted to coheſion, a principle ſo univerſal, that even in ſand it is found ſo ſtrong as to render it, after ſufficient working, water-proof. Where an unmeaſurable weight of water was to be reſiſted, I have ſeen the operation thus performed; a deep perpendicular trench was dug out about four feet wide; in this, as incident to its ſituation, the water ſprung up very plentifully, and into this the ſoil that was raiſed was again returned by degrees, being trampled and beaten, and turned with ſhovels and ſpades, exactly (as I ſaid before)

before) as if it were mortar, by which means it became perfectly viſcous: beyond this point labour is uſeleſs; for attraction has taken place and no more can be added. The practice, on a very confined ſcale, was known before Brindley, but he firſt developed its principles, applied it indiſcriminately to every ſoil, and uſed it to great and extenſive purpoſes, and therefore may juſtly be allowed the honour of having been the inventor.

NOTE K. Page 176.

We ſo ſeldom ſee the rock-work of theſe artificial Caſcades well executed, that perſons of a refined picturesque taſte, are apt to explode them, and to think of them as they do of artificial Ruins and imitative Buildings, that they ought never to be put into execution. Our Author, however, has ventured to recommend both, the one here, and the other in the ſucceeding book; and this, in my opinion, very juſtly, becauſe the arguments againſt their uſe are founded only on that abuſe which has taken away all likeneſs from the imitation; and, ſurely, that they have been ill imitated affords no reaſon that they cannot be well imitated; on the contrary, there is great reaſon to attempt a copy upon better principles, and execute it with truer taſte becauſe there are ſcenes and ſituations in Nature which abſolutely call for ſuch objects to give them their laſt and finiſhed perfection. It is as neceſſary, therefore, for the Gardener to ſupply them upon his living canvaſs, as for the Landſcape Painter to diſplay them upon his dead one; and he is capable of doing this, becauſe he has ſometimes actually done it with full effect.

NOTE XXIII. Verſe 471.

Rejoice; as if the thund'ring Tees himſelf

The fall of the Tees, near Middleton in Yorkſhire, is eſteemed one of the greateſt in England.

NOTE XXIV. Verſe 492.

A Naiad dwells: LINEA *is her name:*

This idea was conceived in a very retired grove at Papplewick in Nottinghamſhire, the ſeat of Frederick Montagu, Eſq; who has long honoured me with his friendſhip, where a little clear trout-ſtream (dignified perhaps too much by the name of a River) gurgles very deliciouſly. This ſtream is called the Lin, and the ſpring itſelf riſes but a little way from his plantations. Hence the name of this Naiad is formed. The village itſelf, which is ſituated on the edge of the foreſt of Sherwood, has not been without poetical notice before, Ben Johnſon having taken ſome of his

Dramatis

Dramatis Personæ from it, in his unfiniſhed Paſtoral Comedy, called *The Sad Shepherd.*

NOTE XXV. Verſe 512.

To Commerce and to Care. In Margaret's grove,

St. John's College in Cambridge, founded by Margaret Counteſs of Richmond, mother of Henry the Seventh.

NOTE XXVI. Verſe 528.

Who ſtole the gift of Thetis. Hence the cauſe,

Alluding to the Ode to a Water Nymph which the Author wrote a year or two after his admiſſion into the univerſity. *See his Poems, Ode* II.

NOTES

UPON

BOOK THE FOURTH

And its COMMENTARY.

NOTE XXVII. Verse 101.

A time-struck Abbey. An impending grove

IT was said in the first Book, ver. 384, that of those architectural objects which improved a fine natural *English* prospect, the two principal were the *Castle* and the *Abbey*. In conformity with this idea, ALCANDER first begins to exercise his taste, by forming a resemblance of those two capital artificial features, *uniting them*, however, *with utility*. The precept is here meant to be conveyed by description, which had before been given more directly in Book II. ver. 21.

> *Beauty* scorns to dwell
> Where *Use* is exil'd.

NOTE

Note L. Page 182.

If we consider how Gothic Edifices were originally constructed, it will appear how very defectively they have been, for the most part, imitated. In order, therefore, to obviate this practice, I will here give a summary and brief description both of such as were Military and Ecclesiastical.

The Gothic Castle, or military structure, consisted in every instance of the Keep or Strong-hold, and the Court or Enclosure annexed to the Keep.

The Keep was a great and high tower, either round or square, for the most part situated on an artificial elevation, the entire top of which it usually occupied. Advantage also was frequently taken of a naturally high situation.

If the tower was square, it often had annexed to it square projections, generally at the corners, and about mid-way between them, to act as buttresses, of which, however, they do not carry the appearance, as they exhibit a front greater than their projection, and do not diminish in their projection as they ascend. When round, I have frequently seen the Keep without any buttress whatever.

The great Portal or door of entrance into the Keep, was always at the least one floor high from the ground, and was usually entered by means of an external staircase

caſe and veſtibule, which was ſtrongly fortified. This ſtair-caſe led only ſo high as the portal, and the landing-place at the head conſiſted for the moſt part of a draw-bridge which was worked from within the Keep, and which, when raiſed, not only cut off all communication, but by leaning againſt and covering the portal, ſerved exceedingly to ſtrenghen it againſt an enemy that might already have taken poſſeſſion of the veſtibule and ſtair-caſe.

There was ſeldom any aperture for a conſiderable height from the ground; and as the apartments of the Lord or Commander of the Caſtle were near the top, it was only there that any aperture appeared which exceeded the ſize of a loop, and even there the windows were of but ſmall dimenſions.

The Keep was uſually embattled at top, but the battlements have in general been defaced by time and ruin.

The wall of the Court, or Encloſure was always connected with the Keep, and the entrance into it was uſually by a great arch ſtrongly fortified, and paſſing between two towers connected by the wall through which the arched-way was carried.—There was never any great arch in the Keep itſelf.

As the wall commenced at the Keep at both ſides, it was commonly carried down the hill, and frequently

quently comprehended not only the defcent but alfo a part of the plain beneath.

The height of the wall, where it joined the Keep, was fometimes regulated by the height of the great portal that led to the principal apartments, which, for the moft part, occupied the third ftory; for the ftair-cafe, by which this was approached, was often built within the fubftance of the wall itfelf, in which cafe there was no other external veftibule.

Loops were frequently made in the wall of the Enclofure; for it was of fuch dimenfions as not only to contain a paffage for maintaining a communication among the parts of the fortrefs within its thicknefs, but had fometimes even apartments either for confinement of prifoners, or for ftores.

The reader, who wifhes for farther information on this fubject, is referred to Mr. King's ingenious and accurate *Obfervations on ancient Caftles.*

Ecclesiastical Buildings, or Abbies, confifted generally of the great Church, a Refectory, a Chapter-Houfe, and a Cloyfter, with the neceffary accommodations of Kitchen, Dormitory, &c.

The Church was ufually in the form of a crofs, in the center of which rofe the tower.—From eaft to weft it was always confiderably longer than from north to fouth.

The

The great weſt end was the place of entrance into the Church; here, therefore, the greateſt degree of ornament was beſtowed both on the portal and the window over it.

The lateral walls were ſtrengthened by buttreſſes which always diminiſhed as they roſe, and between every two windows was a buttreſs.

Within, the inſulated columns ran in rows correſponding with the buttreſſes without.

As a croſs affords two ſides to each of many ſquares, one of theſe ſquares was uſually compleated, and the other two ſides were ſupplied, the one by the cloyſter, which was frequently carried in length from north to ſouth, and the other by the refectory and chapter-houſe, which ſtood at right angles with this cloyſter, and parallel to the body of the Church from eaſt to weſt.

The cloyſter was ſometimes carried into length, and ſometimes ſurrounded a ſquare court; over the cloyſter was the cuſtomary place for the dormitory.

None of the parts of the Abbey at all approached to the height of the Church.

The great pointed arch was an invention ſubſequent to the building of many Abbies, which have ſmall round-topped windows; theſe, therefore, may very well be placed in the ſides of the Church; but in the

weſt

weſt end, for the moſt part, the pointed arch was introduced as a high ornament by ſucceeding Architects.

There never yet was built an external column; nor an internal buttreſs; miniature imitations of theſe were indeed promiſcuouſly introduced among the ſmaller ornaments of the building; but the rule is invariably true with regard to the great ſtructure itſelf.

The ſtone-work of Gothic buildings was very neatly hewn and jointed; and even now their very ruins are by no means rough on the ſurface, except in the immediate neighbourhood of the ſpot where time has made a breach, or where they have been ſtripped of their caſing.

Though the rules of Gothic Architecture have not been ſo diligently inquired into as thoſe of the Greek, yet certain we may be, from the reſemblance which prevails, not only in the whole, but in the parts of all great Gothic edifices among themſelves, that they were conſtructed upon rules which it would be better for us to inveſtigate than diſpenſe with in favour of the ſilly caprices which we daily ſee executed under the name of GOTHIC BUILDINGS, to the diſgrace of our Obſervation and Taſte. I have ſeen a Gothic

Temple, an open Gothic Portico, a Gothic Cupola, and I have seen an arched Gothic Rotunda!

Magnitude is a *sine quâ non* of Gothic Architecture.

I have been forced to make use of the qualifying terms *usually*, *for the most part*, *&c.* because I cannot say that any of these rules, tho' general, are without, perhaps, many exceptions. I am writing, not for the benefit of the Gothic Architect, but his picturesque Imitator, for whom these few precepts and cautions, I trust, will be found sufficiently precise.

The reader will not suppose, that by thus delineating the rules by which these two sorts of edifices were constructed, I recommend to the imitator an exact copy of the whole of either, much less that I would wish him to execute on a small scale what can only have probability when practised on a great one. I only require a judicious selection of the parts of such buildings, and that each may be made with exactness to occupy its proper place. A remnant of the Keep, of the great gate of entrance, or even of a single tower, with an additional length of ruined wall, will frequently answer the purpose of imitation in the military style very completely, while a single high-arched window or portal, a part of a low groyned cloyster, and a few mutilated columns justly arranged within the supposed body of the Church, will equally well answer

anſwer it in the eccleſiaſtical ſtyle: But the general faults that have prevailed in theſe kinds of imitation is, firſt, that of deſigning too much, perhaps a whole; ſecondly, the executing that whole upon a pigmy ſcale; thirdly, the introduction of a capricious mode of ornament; and, laſtly, a total neglect of the real poſition of the parts. The beſt, perhaps the only good rule that can be followed, is to copy ſome beautiful fragment of an antient ruin with the ſame fidelity that one would copy a portrait, and happily for our purpoſe England abounds with ſuch fragments; but let us ever avoid invention where our proper buſineſs is only imitation.

The deſcription of Alcander's manſion remarkably coincides with Leland the Antiquary's account of Greenwich in its antient ſtate.

Ecce ut jam niteat locus petitus,
Tanquam ſydereæ domus cathedræ!
Quæ faſtigia picta! quæ feneſtræ!
Quæ turres vel ad aſtra ſe efferentes!

Κυκνειον Ἀσμα, ver. 310.

Leland died A. D. 1552.

Note XXVIII. Verse 131.

And fright the local Genius from the scene.

A precept is here rather more than hinted at; but it appeared to be so well founded, and yet so seldom attended to by the fabricators of Grottos, that it seemed necessary to slide back a little from the narrative into the didactic to inculcate it the more strongly.

Note XXIX. Verse 157.

His Galatea: Yes, th' impassion'd Youth

Alluding to a Letter of that famous Painter, written to his Friend Count Baltasar Castiglione, when he was painting his celebrated picture of Galatea, in which he tells him, *essendo carestia di belle donne, io mi servo di certa idea che viene alla mente.* See Bellori *Discriz. delle imagini dipinte da Raffaelle d'Urbino*, or the Life of B. Castiglione, prefixt to the London Edition of his Book entitled, *Il Cortegiano.*

Note XXX. Verse 201.

Irregular, yet not in patches quaint,

There is nothing in picturesque Gardening which should not have its archetype in unadorned Nature. Now, as we never see any of her plains dotted with dissevered patches of any sort of vegetables, except, perhaps, some of her more barren heaths, where even

Furze

Furze can grow but ſparingly, and which form the moſt diſagreeable of her ſcenes; therefore the preſent common mode of dotting clumps of flowers, or ſhrubs on a graſs-plot, without union, and without other meaning than that of appearing irregular, ought to be avoided. It is the form and eaſy flow of the graſſy interſtices (if I may ſo call them) that the deſigner ought firſt to have a regard to; and if theſe be well formed, the ſpaces for flowers or ſhrubbery will be at the ſame time aſcertained.

NOTE XXXI. Verſe 218.

Might ſafely flouriſh; where the Citron ſweet,

M. Le Giradin, in an elegant French Eſſay, written on the ſame ſubject, and formed on the ſame principles, with this Poem, is the only writer that I have ſeen (or at leaſt recollect) who has attempted to give a ſtove or hot-houſe a pictureſque effect. It is his hint, purſued and conſiderably dilated, which forms the deſcription of ALCANDER's Conſervatory. See his Eſſay, *De la compoſition des Payſages. Gen.* 1777.

NOTE XXXII. Verſe 358.

The Linnets warble, captive none, but lur'd

See Rouſſeau's charming deſcription of the Garden of Julie, *Nouvelle Eloiſe*, 4 *partie*, *lett.* 11*th*. In

conſequence

consequence of pursuing his idea, no birds are introduced into ALCANDER's Menagerie, but such as are either domesticated, or chuse to visit it for the security and food they find there. If any of my more delicate readers wish to have theirs stocked with rarer kind of fowls, they must invent a picturesque Bird-cage for themselves.

NOTE XXXIII. Verse 427.

Till, like fatigu'd VILLARIO, *soon we find*

See Pope's Epistle to Lord Burlington, ver. 88.

NOTE XXXIV. Verse 448.

Tho' foreign from the soil, provokes thy frown.

It is hoped that, from the position of this River-God in the menagerie; from the situation of the busts and vases in the flower-garden; and that of the statue in the conservatory, the reader will deduce the following general precept, "that all adventitious ornaments of sculpture ought either to be accompanied with a proper back-ground (as the Painters term it) or introduced as a part of architectural scenery; and that when, on the contrary, they are placed in open lawns or parterres, according to the old mode, they become, like Antæus and Enceladus mentioned in the beginning of this book, mere *scare-crows*."

NOTE

Note XXXV. Verse 462.

"*If true, here only.*" *Thus, in Milton's phrase*

See Milton's Paradise Lost, b. iv. ver. 248, &c.

Note XXXVI. Verse 499.

To those that tend the dying. Both the youths

These lines are taken from the famous passage in Hippocrates in his book of Prognostics, which has been held so accurately descriptive, that dying persons are, from hence, usually said to have the *facies Hippocratica.* The passage is as follow: Ῥὶς ὀξεῖα, ὀφθαλμοὶ κοῖλοι, κρόταφοι ξυμπεπτωκότες, ὦτα ψυχρὰ καὶ ξυνεσταλμένα, καὶ οἱ λόβοι τῶν ὤτων ἀπεστραμμένοι, καὶ τὸ δέρμα τὸ περὶ τὸ μέτωπον, σκληρὸν τε καὶ περιτεταμένον καὶ καρφαλέον ἐὸν, καὶ τὸ χρῶμα τοῦ ξύμπαντος προσώπου χλωρὸν τε ἢ καὶ μέλαν ἐὸν καὶ πελιὸν ἢ μολιβδῶδες.

Note XXXVII. Verse 646.

He bids them raise: it seem'd a Hermit's cell;

If this building is found to be in its right position, structures of the same kind will be thought improperly placed when situated, as they frequently are, on an eminence commanding an extensive prospect. I have either seen or heard of one of this kind, where the builder seemed to be so much convinced of its incongruity, that he endeavoured to atone for it by the following ingenious motto:

Despicere

Despicere unde queas alios, passimque videre
Errare, atque viam palanteis quærere vitæ.

Luc. lib. ii. v. 9.

But it may be said, that real Hermitages are frequently found on high mountains: Yet there the difficulty of access gives that idea of retirement, not easily to be conveyed by imitations of them in a Garden-scene, without much accompanying shade and that lowness of situation, which occasions a seclusion from all gay objects

Note M. Page 187.

Cicero has beautifully expressed a similar sentiment in the following terms:

Tum Piso: Naturâne nobis hoc datum, dicam, an errore quodam, ut cum ea loca videamus, in quibus Memoriâ dignos viros acceperimus multos esse versatos, magis moveamur, quam siquando eorum ipsorum aut facta audiamus, aut scriptum aliquod legamus? velut ego nunc moveor: venit enim mihi Platonis (memoria *sc.*) in mentem, quem acceperimus primum hîc (in Academia *sc.*) disputare solitum: cujus etiam illi hortuli propinqui non memoriam solûm mihi afferunt sed ipsum videntur in conspectu meo hîc ponere; hîc Speusippus, hîc Xenocrates, hîc ejus auditor Polemo; cujus ipsa illa sessio fuit quam videmus—tanta vis admonitionis

monitionis ineſt in locis ut non ſine causâ ex his memoriæ ducta ſit diſciplina.—*Cicero de Fin.* lib. v. *ad init. (vide quoque quod ibid. de Carneade idem dicit.)*

My buſineſs, as an illuſtrator of the Engliſh Garden, properly ends here; but as the Author thought fit, in a general Poſtſcript to the firſt edition of his Poem, not only to aſſign his reaſons for compoſing this fourth Book, in a ſtyle ſo different from thoſe that go before it, but to defend the particular Tale, in which he has conveyed his precepts, in a manner that I think reflects as much honour upon his heart, as the deſign and conduct of the Story does upon his invention and judgment, I chuſe here to reprint the two paragraphs for the mere ſatisfaction of declaring my own concurrence with the ſentiments they convey.

"Though this ſubject was in itſelf as ſuſceptible of poetical embelliſhment as any that preceded it, and much more ſo than thoſe contained in the ſecond book; yet I was apprehenſive that deſcriptive poetry, however varied, might pall when continued through ſo long a poem; and therefore, by interweaving a Tale with the general theme, I have given the whole a narrative, and in ſome places a dramatic caſt. The idea was new, and I found the execution

 of

of it ſomewhat difficult: However, if I have ſo far ſucceeded as to have conveyed, through the medium of an intereſting ſtory, thoſe more important principles of taſte which this part of my ſubject required, and if thoſe rules only are omitted which readily reſult from ſuch as I have deſcriptively given; if the judicious place and arrangement of thoſe artificial forms, which give the chief embelliſhment to a finiſhed garden-ſcene, be diſtinctly noticed, I am not without hope that this concluſion will be thought (as Sir Henry Wotton ſaid of Milton's juvenile Poems at the end of a miſcellany) to leave the reader in ſome ſmall degree *con la bocca dolce.*

With reſpect to the criticiſms, which may be made on this laſt book, there is one ſo likely to come from certain readers, that I am inclined to anticipate it; and taking for granted that it will be ſaid to breathe too much of the ſpirit of party, to return the following ready anſwer: The word *Party*, when applied to thoſe men, who, from private and perſonal motives, compoſe either a majority or minority in a houſe of parliament, or to thoſe who out of it, on ſimilar principles, approve or condemn the meaſures of any adminiſtration, is certainly in its place: But in a matter of ſuch magnitude as the preſent Ameri-

can

can War, in which the dearest interests of mankind are concerned, the puny term has little or no meaning. If, however, it be applied to me on this occasion, I shall take it with much complacency, conscious that no sentiment appears in my Poem which does not prove its author to be of THE PARTY OF HUMANITY."

F I N I S.

www.ingramcontent.com/pod-product-compliance
Lightning Source LLC
Chambersburg PA
CBHW020852270326
41928CB00006B/659

* 9 7 8 3 7 4 4 7 7 1 4 8 1 *